Greek Mythology

Discover the Epic Stories, Heroes, and Deities That Shaped Ancient Greece

Table of Contents

Introduction

Ever since consciousness evolved past a point that allowed people to ask existential questions, the inherent human attribute of problem-solving has been directed at more than mere survival. Indeed, the human ability to solve problems has helped early humanity survive, thrive, and eventually build complex societies, resolving many of the practical issues of life on this planet. However, as sophisticated as this ability is, it would always encounter insurmountable obstacles whenever people tried to resolve existential quandaries.

The existential questions that have consistently occupied the human mind have mostly revolved around the issues of how and why in relation to the origins of the universe, humanity, and consciousness itself. Another persistent object of wonder that has titillated people's imagination since time immemorial has been natural phenomena. Understanding all these things, long before the advent of modern science, has always involved a unique form of problem-solving that went beyond what is immediately observable.

Seeing as religion has never failed to emerge across civilizations with no contact with each other. It's clear that humans have a very natural curiosity and almost a primal need to answer these higher questions. For much of history and across civilizations, this important task was assigned to philosophers of various methods and doctrines. In some form or another, every developed civilization has tried its hand at unlocking the most glaring existential mysteries and understanding the natural world around them.

From the primitive attempts in prehistoric times to more complex societies that came later, many such attempts have probably been lost to time. Others have been preserved thanks to oral tradition, written records, artifacts, and other heritage that can now be studied as a window into the past. Apart from the popular religions that are widespread across the world today, Greek mythology stands as one of the most preserved and studied human endeavors pursuant to explaining the nature of the universe.

Renowned for their affinity for philosophy and other intellectual feats, the ancient Greeks developed a fascinating system of religious practices, beliefs, myths, legends, stories, and folklore. The ancient Greek religion was the centerpiece of philosophy, spiritual life, and worldly understanding in ancient Greece, but Greek mythology produced much more than religious practice and dogma. It's a collection of myths that permeated oral traditions, rituals, politics, poetry, other literature, and much more. These myths, as told by the Greeks, made comments on the nature of the world by using intricate stories revolving around all sorts of deities, legendary heroes, and mythical creatures.

Such stories worked as individual parts of a greater whole. The famous pantheon of Greek gods and goddesses was, in itself, an incredibly intricate narrative that offered explanations about the world by delving into the lives, relationships, and personalities of the deities that ruled it.

Many ancient Greek deities functioned as personifications of certain natural phenomena, having well-developed personalities and a rather human face on the surface. In fact, many of the stories that the ancient Greeks told about their deities were strikingly human in their themes and characters.

The anthropomorphism of these deities went far beyond their physical appearance, as shown in artistic depictions. Even though they were seen as immortal and unfathomably powerful, Greek gods weren't infallible and flawless, nor were they always benevolent. They exhibited traits and emotions like vindictiveness, lust, love, hatred, cunning, kindness, cruelty, infatuation with power, and many other characteristics that are widely present among mortals. In the stories, Greek gods fought wars, struggled, rebelled, ruled, and worked both with and against one another. As such, ancient Greek religion explored the human condition just as much as natural phenomena.

Many of the stories served as cautionary tales and moral lessons, significantly influencing the way the ancient Greeks lived their daily lives, conducted politics, and waged war. That's one of the reasons why contemporary historical records, interpretations, and retellings in ancient Greece were so intimately interwoven with mythology. This is best exemplified by the legendary Trojan War, which the ancient Greeks believed to have taken place around the 13th and 12th centuries BC. This epic story has been retold across ancient Greek literature such as Homer's *Odyssey* and *Iliad* and other epic poems. It is presented as a historical event while featuring tales of legendary heroes such as Achilles, who was essentially a demigod.

By the 19th century, it was widely believed that the story of the Trojan War was completely mythological, but this belief has been challenged more recently, thanks to archeological discoveries that suggest that the city of Troy had indeed existed. These discoveries imply that the chronicles of the war might have been based on an actual event and thoroughly mythologized over the subsequent centuries. The construction of a complex mythological story around a basic historical crux would illustrate perfectly how the ancient Greeks treated their myths and historiography with equal reverence. By weaving the two together to create a powerful thread of oral and written tradition, the Greeks would have maintained a vivid and unbreakable bond with their ancestors.

Apart from legendary heroes, deities, and their lives and origins, Greek myths delved into many other common burning questions of human reality. As always, what happens after death was an area of keen interest for the ancient Greeks. Greek mythology also grappled with the origins of humanity in both practical and existential terms. While mythology was highly regarded as an integral part of tradition, culture, art, and spirituality, it should be noted that the ancient Greeks probably held a wide range of views on these concepts. It's untrue that every ancient Greek person, let alone a scholar, took these myths at face value and interpreted them as a literal account of world history.

As is the case with today's religions, many observers would have probably seen a lot of the mythology as metaphorical.

Some folks in ancient Greece were skeptical of mainstream religion while others lived by it, but all understood the body of Greek myths to be an important aspect of heritage, culture, philosophy, and art. Greek mythology was incredibly influential in art and literature of the day, and this influence has persisted across time and distance. The initial spread, mainly through oral tradition, likely began in the 18th century BC with the Minoans from Crete and Mycenaean Greeks. It is unclear how strictly the subsequent retellings followed certain rules and formats, but the ensuing centuries undoubtedly brought a degree of adaptation and mixture of local influences as the Greek city-states became more inter-connected.

The advent of poetry in Ionia in western Anatolia and the legendary writings of Homer and Hesiod in the 8th century BC were pivotal in developing Greek mythology further and preserving it. Up to this point, the depiction of myths and stories in written form was uncommon, so a lot of what is known about Greek mythology from contemporary sources comes from this period. Homer's *Iliad* and *Odyssey* offer a look into Greek mythology as it interprets history. On the other hand, Hesiod explained the origin and rise of Greek deities in the *Theogony* and the emergence of humanity in his *Works and Days.*

These writings provide a detailed account of man and gods and highlight that legendary Greek heroes were a sort of bridge between the two, as they were usually born of one human and one divine parent. Also, around the 8th century BC, Greek pottery started to feature a growing number of mythological scenes, which have provided archeologists with valuable insights. A couple of centuries later, philosophers preceding Socrates began to approach the myths with more skepticism and some even denied them entirely. These were the early attempts to unlock the mysteries of history with a more scientific lens. Such efforts gave rise to new schools of thought in the 5th century BC, at which point work by the likes of Thucydides and Herodotus spawned the intellectual exercise of history as it's understood today.

Around the same time, Greek mythology became deeply entrenched in Greek comedies and tragedies as literature proliferated. Despite the eventual decline of Greek mythology in everyday life, its strong presence in art, literature, and culture would never stop. In fact, it would only expand until these myths and traditions became an integral part of Western heritage as a whole. Ancient Greeks were also known to have heavily influenced the Romans, with the polytheistic Roman religion adopting many of the same gods, albeit under different names. The famous Roman foundation myth of Romulus and Remus also references Troy, highlighting the Roman fascination with Greek literature.

Greek myths spoke of the gods and the universe in such human terms that the themes in the stories are essentially timeless, inspiring writers, philosophers, and artists to this very day. This book will provide a detailed overview of all major facets of Greek mythology, helping the reader grasp its full scope and the reasons why ancient Greece is seen by many as the progenitor of Western civilization.

Chapter 1: The Cosmos and the Gods

If Greek mythology was to be taken as a chronological narrative, it would start with a creation myth. As in most other religions, the religion of the ancient Greeks had quite a few things to say about the creation of the universe and the emergence of the many deities and mythological creatures it spoke of. Humanity and the observable natural world also join the tale at a later point, but a major portion of Greek polytheism is devoted to the divine realm. Stretching across the ages, it is a story featuring many different characters, their complex personalities and relationships, and their struggles. In a way, generational struggle is one of the central themes, as Greek mythology begins by describing a universe that materialized and existed long before the Greek pantheon of deities emerged and took over.

Theogony: Origins of the Gods and Goddesses

Much of what is understood about the ancient Greek view on the origins of the universe and their creation myth as a whole comes from Hesiod's *Theogony*. The *Theogony* is a piece of ancient poetry that originates in the 8th century BC. It is essentially an instructional poem that chronicles the creation of the universe, the birth of the primordial gods, and the eventual war between these first beings and the Olympian deities. It describes the early ages of the universe as a period of both creation and chaos, with generational conflict and succession playing one of the central roles.

Another fascinating characteristic of the *Theogony* is that it also comments on the state of the universe before creation.

This piece of literature originated as an oral tradition like most aspects of Greek mythology. Such oral traditions often took the form of singing and other narrative performances, which were the main mode of passing down cultural heritage before literacy proliferated across the ancient Greek states. The title *Theogony* is derived from the Greek word "theogonia," which translates as "generations of the gods." Consisting of over 1,000 lines, the *Theogony* is an impressive piece of epic poetry that covers a hefty story.

Hesiod most likely finished putting the *Theogony* together around 700 BC. Unsurprisingly, for a poet from so long ago, there is a lot of mystery surrounding Hesiod. He most likely spent a lot of his life as a farmer and, at some point, engaged in recitals. This would have probably helped him to learn the techniques needed for poetry and deepened his creative interest, so he eventually went on to compose his own poems. Due to all the uncertainties about Hesiod and his life, some historians have questioned his authorship of the *Theogony* over the years, but these suggestions haven't gained much traction.

The authorship issue hasn't been too hotly debated because Hesiod, after all, was but a skilled composer of already existing oral traditions, which he so eloquently compiled but didn't necessarily write. The poem was credited to Hesiod and passed down, but it was put to writing decades later, so it's possible that the *Theogony* has absorbed certain additions in that period and especially over the following centuries. Hesiod's other important piece, *Works and Days*, probably came later because, as historians like Dorothea Wender have noted, it exhibits a higher quality and appears more polished.

There are notable distinctions in how Hesiod and Homer described the gods, particularly in regard to their virtues. Homer's work gave the gods many attributes that closely resembled well-known human flaws, but the realm of the gods was still characterized by a degree of order. Hesiod's poetry featured much less whitewashing of mythology, as Wender put it, with the notable exception of Zeus, who was the main protagonist in the story. Hesiod's grittier approach could have been influenced by the target audience, as Homer's poetry was more directed toward the upper classes that preferred refined depictions of deities. Hesiod likely didn't have such aims, so his descriptions of divine narratives featured more chaos and primitivism regarding the ways of the world and the behavior of gods.

The *Theogohy* begins with some comments on how Hesiod became interested in poetry and singing. The initial lines tell a short story of the nine Muses who approached Hesiod when he was herding sheep and taught him the ways of poetry and performance. Hesiod also explained that the Muses told him to tell the tales of the immortals, and they also bestowed upon him knowledge about what had happened before the emergence of the universe. The central part of that story was the birth of Zeus, his early life, and how he ultimately overthrew his father Cronus (also known as Cronos and Kronos), who had previously overthrown his own father, Uranus (Ouranos). This theme constitutes the essential succession myth in ancient Greek religion, but it also chronicles the Greek cosmogony myth via personification of the world's many integral parts.

A particularly striking aspect of the *Theogony* is the brutality of the gods in their various affairs, especially succession. The castration of Uranus by the sickle of Cronus, coupled with the latter's eventual devouring of his own offspring, left a lasting impact on Greek mythology and the art it inspired over the centuries. Hesiod's portrayal of the gods, except the heroic Zeus, is often horrendous. These dark presentations in both Hesiod's and Homer's works were commented on in ancient times as well. Xenophanes of Colophon, an ancient Greek philosopher who lived roughly between 570 and 478 BC, noted that these old epics had a tendency to take shameful and disgraceful manifestations of human behavior and attribute them to the gods. In contrast, Hesiod's interpretation of Zeus exalted his penchant for justice and courage, treating him as the final word and peak in the creation and stabilization of the cosmos. He is also described as omniscient, much like the Abrahamic god.

As per the main narrative in the *Theogony,* the cosmogony of Greek mythology begins before the birth of the first gods, back when the universe was in a chaotic state. In Hesiod's portrayals, Chaos was personified to an extent like other deities, but he also symbolized a dark, formless void. In this context, the Greek term better translates as "Chasm" or "Abyss" than as the English word "chaos." This primordial state didn't have the connotations that the English term carriers, such as disorder or confusion, and is instead more akin to an abyss of nothingness. Chaos was both an entity and a place, with its most anthropomorphic ability being that of bearing children, so to speak.

Chaos was essentially the first thing in all of existence, after which came Gaia (Earth), Eros (Universal Love, Desire, Passion), and Tartarus (Underworld). There's some debate as to whether these three materialized spontaneously or were born to Chaos, but there is no question that Chaos came first. The undisputed "children" of Chaos were Nyx (Night) and Erebus (Darkness), who were born spontaneously and without a partner. Gaia, or Earth, was noted for her fertility, which allowed her to bear many children without a spouse through a version of immaculate conception.

Metaphorically speaking, Gaia birthed the different essential parts of the world as perceived by humanity. As the Muses revealed to Hesiod in the poem, "the broad-breasted Earth, the ever-safe foundation of all the deathless ones who live on the peaks of snowy Olympos," came right after Chaos. The primordial gods, such as Tartarus and Eros, had no physical form like the later gods, and although they came after Chaos, they are also described as having existed since the beginning of time.

Chaos, Gaia, Uranus, and the Titans

The next of the primordial gods came from Erebus and the goddess Nyx, who gave birth to Aether and Hemera. Aether personified brightness, radiance, or light, while Hemera represented day. As such, Aether and Hemera were the opposite of their parents' nature, symbolizing night and darkness. Nyx would bear many other offspring, and her children are the perfect example of just how many aspects of human life were represented by deities in Greek mythology. The many children of Nyx, most in some way associated with the night or darkness, symbolized things like destiny, doom, death, sleep, hypnosis, blame, pain, retribution, discord, dreams, and much more.

At the same time, the mother goddess Gaia's fertility gave rise to many new creations, including monstrous ones like Typhon. Typhon was the most enormous monstrosity ever to emerge from the depths of the abyss, born as a result of Gaia's coupling with Tartarus. In turn, Typhon went on to beget many other abominations with Echidna, who herself was a serpent-like monster born to sea gods. One of these creatures was Cerberus, the three-headed, dog-like beast that stood guard at the gates of the underworld. This was how the key worldly elements of earth, night, day, and love, in addition to various monsters, materialized in the universe, according to Hesiod's *Theogony*.

One of the most important steps in the ancient Greek cosmogony happened when Gaia birthed Uranus, which essentially began the main line of succession. Uranus (Heaven or Sky) enveloped Gaia from all sides, and thus Heaven and Earth came together to form many other things in the world, but not before Gaia had more children on her own. These included the nymphs of the woods, Pontus (Sea), Ourea (Mountains), and many others. Having birthed the sky, the mountains, and the sea and thus giving shape to the world, Gaia decided to start bearing children with a partner. She joined with her son Uranus in what could be described as a divine marriage, and among their children were the famous twelve Titans, or rather the first Titan generation. Many of the Titans would marry among themselves in sibling unions and produce their own children.

Oceanus was the eldest of the Titans and of all the children of Gaia and Uranus. Similarly to Pontus, Oceanus was closely related to the seas and oceans, but he was represented as a great river that enveloped the entire world. Oceanus is sometimes referred to as the Ocean River due to its personification of all the seas, oceans, and adjacent rivers. As such, he was the source of all rivers known to man, which were likened to a number of smaller river gods, including the Nile and the Styx. Oceanus also fathered three thousand benevolent nymphs known as the Oceanids.

The rest of the twelve Titans included Coeus, Crius, Hyperion, Iapetus, Mnemosyne, Rhea, Phoebe, Tethys, Theia, Themis, and the infamous Cronus, described as the "crooked" or "scheming Kronos." Apart from the first-generation Titans, Heaven and Earth also brought Cyclopes and the Giants into the world. Hesiod's Cyclopes were formidable, fearsome, one-eyed creatures, including Brontes, Arges, and Steropes. The Giants were also a trio called the Hecatoncheires, and they included Kottos, Gyes, and Briareus. All three were enormous beings, each with a hundred hands and fifty heads.

Further solidifying her moniker of the mother goddess were the children Gaia had with Pontus. These included deities such as Phorcys, Ceto, Thaumas, and Eurybia. In general, all of the most important deities of Greek mythology are children or descendants of Gaia, which gives her an attribute of supremacy and reverence among other gods and goddesses and humanity. When the mythology and its endless metaphors and symbolism are unpacked, the ancient Greek cosmogony becomes rather simple. It's the story of Heaven (Uranus), Earth (Gaia), and Sea (Pontus) coming together to form everything else in the world that people can observe with their eyes or experience and feel in their hearts and minds.

As Gaia represents Earth, her motherly figure is most fitting, as is the adoration she enjoyed among mortals and immortals. The motherly theme is passed down from Gaia through her Titan daughter Rhea, who was also hailed as a mother goddess. Her importance was perhaps equal to that of Gaia because it was through her and her offspring that the eventual pantheon of the twelve Olympians, who were the main objects of Greek worship, came to be. As a supreme motherly figure, Gaia was generally seen as a benevolent figure and a caring parental goddess, in stark contrast to her main partner, Uranus. A similar theme would mark the eternal lives and progeny of Rhea and her brother-husband Cronus.

Indeed, the relationship between Uranus and his children is where the *Theogony's* dark portrayal of the gods truly begins to make itself known. The story also establishes the important theme of brutal, unceremonious successions and some terribly troubled father-son dynamics. Uranus was portrayed as a god who loved his power and generally hated his children. Titans, Cyclopes, and Giants alike were all unable to escape his scorn, which was an unsettling state of affairs for Gaia. Uranus manifested his disdain for his offspring by having them hidden away underground, which could be interpreted as within Gaia, with the idea of keeping them out of his sight.

Eventually, Gaia decided she would no longer tolerate her husband's ways and began to hatch a plan for his demise. Hesiod's *Theogony* refers to it as a "clever, evil plan" and describes how Gaia made a powerful adamantine sickle to be used to castrate Uranus. She presented her plan to her children but took no joy in it, lamenting that their father was a "reckless fool" who needed to answer for his "wicked crime," all while feeling "sorrow in her heart" over the whole predicament and stressing that it was Uranus who had brought it on himself. Their sons and daughters were afraid of Uranus, however, and none but Cronus, who was Gaia's youngest, dared step out of line.

There are a number of interpretations as to how Cronus ambushed his father, but the crux of the narrative is that Gaia helped hide Cronus. Cronus then waited patiently until Uranus came around to couple with Gaia, at which point Cronus emerged from hiding and severed his father's genitals. Cronus then threw his father's member into the sea, and as he did, the blood from it fell on Gaia, thus raining down on Earth. This blood sowed the seeds from which the Furies, or the goddesses of vengeance, sprouted. Where the organ fell and hit the water, the sea began to foam and boil, giving rise to Aphrodite, the famed goddess of love, lust, and much else. As a result of this defeat, Uranus relinquished his power to Cronus.

After assuming the throne, Cronus married his sister Rhea. His triumph came with an ominous warning from his parents, who prophesized that he, too, would eventually be deposed by one of his sons. His thirst for power and perhaps his trauma from having dealt with his own father in such a brutal fashion made Cronus horribly paranoid. The *Theogony* takes one of its darkest turns in this part of the story, chronicling how Cronus would consume every son birthed by Rhea as a prophylactic measure. Cronus, known to the Romans as Saturn, is remembered across the world, especially for devouring his sons – a terrible crime portrayed and adapted many times throughout history by various artists.

The Rise of Zeus and the Olympian Gods

When people talk about the Greek gods nowadays, they're usually referring to the Olympian pantheon, also known as the twelve Olympians. Their rise to greatness and rule over the world came through struggle and would represent the final order in the universe, even though they were far from being the first deities. Their story begins with tormented Rhea making the fateful decision to put an end to Cronus' beastly methods of staying in power. When each of Rhea's sons was born, Cronus would have her bring him over to be eaten, but by the time she had conceived Zeus, Rhea was at the end of her wits.

She confided in Gaia about her suffering, telling her that she was pregnant with Zeus and wanted to find a way to save him from Cronus. Moved by Rhea's predicament, Gaia proposed that she should run away to the island of Crete, where she could safely give birth to Zeus and have him hidden in a cave. Gaia also instructed Rhea to locate a particular stone, which would later be used as a decoy to fool Cronus. Upon her arrival in Crete, Rhea was also assisted by Amalthea, the she-goat and nymphs known as the Maliae.

Back home, Rhea feigned a birth and informed Cronus that a new son was born. She then handed her husband the stone wrapped in a blanket to resemble an infant, which Cronus quickly swallowed, oblivious to the ploy. Rhea then hurried back to Crete and gave birth to Zeus, after which she vowed that he would exact his mother's vengeance on Cronus, thus allowing the cycle of troubled succession to continue. After the birth, Rhea left Zeus in the care of her helpers and returned home to continue her life. It was also Gaia who took upon herself a lot of the work required to raise Zeus.

According to the *Theogony,* Zeus was born in Lyktos and hidden in a cave on Mount Aegaeon. Authors other than Hesiod have suggested a few different locations as the birthplace of Zeus, but the overall theme of a cave and mount in Crete prevails. As Zeus was growing up, Rhea would visit him regularly and ensure he would receive the training he needed to destroy his father one day. Zeus grew up into a powerful god, and as he reached his peak, the conspirators finalized their plans. Rhea and Metis, one of the Oceanid nymphs and eventually Zeus' first wife, created a powerful potion that Zeus would use to defeat Cronus.

The potion wasn't a poison, however. Zeus ensured that his father drank it so that he would vomit out all of Zeus' siblings whom he had swallowed. These gods, following the recently swallowed stone, included Poseidon, Hades, Hera, Demeter, and Hestia, thrown up by Cronus in that sequence. After his children were released from his abdominal prison, Cronus lost consciousness. The opportunity to finish the matter right then and there was missed because Zeus couldn't muster up the strength to swing his sickle and behead Cronus. Nonetheless, he walked out of this first encounter with the sworn allegiance of his grateful siblings. Thus, the alliance that would bring about the era of the Olympian gods was formed.

Cronus wasn't willing to just roll over and surrender, though, and so began the Titanomachy. This was a ten-year war between the Titans and the Olympians, with the Olympians operating from their eponymous mountain while the Titans were based on Mount Othrys. It was a long and grueling battle that shook the cosmos and the known world, with the Olympians initially outmatched and outnumbered. The narrative then evolves into a story of triumph through strategy and cooperation, with a subtle sheen of *deus ex machina*.

The turning point in the war came when Zeus, following the wise counsel of Metis, descended to Tartarus and released the Cyclopes and the Giants to employ as allies in the struggle against the Titans. Having been continuously imprisoned by Uranus, the creatures were grateful and willing to lend a helping hand. The Cyclopes provided much more than muscle, as they were the designers of many of the famous Olympian weapons and powers. These included the legendary thunderbolts commanded by Zeus, Poseidon's trident, and other tools that would turn the tide against Cronus. The Giants, with their many hands, were also formidable in battle.

Under pressure, the Titans elected Atlas to lead them in battle. Despite the commendable resistance of the Titans under Atlas' leadership, the Olympian onslaught ultimately proved unstoppable. Another decisive factor, as per the *Theogony,* was the unbridled rage of Zeus, which escalated as the war went on. Once Zeus "no longer checked his rage," he was finally able to unleash "the full range of his strength."

Once the Titans were crushed, they were banished into the depths of Tartarus as punishment. As for their field commander Atlas, Zeus was not content to merely banish him and instead condemned him to forever hold up the heavens on his shoulders. Different sources have given a few varying accounts of Cronus' fate after the war. Some say he was punished with the impossible task of measuring eternity and also made to gradually age, which led to his later interpretation as Father Time. Other portrayals talk of banishment to Tartarus with the other Titans.

Following their victory, the Olympians assumed control over the underworld (Hades), the seas (Poseidon), the heavens (Zeus), and other parts of reality. Zeus was also crowned king of the gods and would forever rule from his throne on Mount Olympus. The rest of the main Olympian gods, who were not his siblings or Aphrodite, would come later as his progeny.

The ancient Greek cosmogony and its consequences, as outlined in the *Theogony* and other scripts, comprise a very complex narrative. These stories abound in symbols, metaphors, and many layers, which is why they've been unpacked, analyzed, and interpreted for thousands of years. There are intense discussions to be had about these interpretations, particularly because the aforementioned deities and concepts tended to represent almost all the sights and experiences a person would encounter during their lifetime.

The concept of vengeance, for instance, was perhaps purposely tied to the retribution exacted by a son on his hateful father. Similarly, the fact that this primordial vengeance was carried out by Cronus, himself a hateful deity who devoured his own children, is perhaps also not accidental. Furthermore, the blood spilled during Cronus' revenge birthed, among others, the goddess of lust, passion, and beauty, as personified by Aphrodite. This could have been an ancient poet's way of commenting on the temporary emotional satisfaction born of a passionate, heated moment of revenge before the act eventually leads the protagonist down a dark path.

The subsequent paranoia of Cronus over meeting the same fate at the hands of others, which drove him to unspeakable atrocities against his own sons, is also an interesting symbol to ponder. It could be interpreted as a psychological projection, particularly that of a criminal on the perpetual lookout in anticipation of having done unto him that which he had done unto others. These examples merely scratch the surface of the lessons and debates that *Theogony* and overall Greek mythology have brought up, inspiring countless curious and creative minds in the process.

Chapter 2: The Olympian Pantheon

While the twelve Olympians formed the core of worship and sacrifice in ancient Greece, it's important to note that they were complemented by other major deities that aren't generally included among the Olympians. Hades, the famous ruler of the underworld and the god of the dead is a perfect example of this. Hades was a brother to Zeus and the first-generation Olympians, but he is excluded from the main twelve-part pantheon because his dominion in the underworld was far removed from Olympus.

Deities like Hades are usually classified as Chthonic gods, which is a term derived from the ancient Greek word for soil or earth, with a connotation of "under" or "beneath the earth." Among classicists, there is usually a contrast between Chthonic and Olympian deities. The canonical twelve Olympians almost perfectly represent the important role that ancient Greek polytheism played in all human affairs and daily life since they tend to personify most of the main features of the ancient Greek experience. Apart from the stories already mentioned, there is much else that sets these gods apart from each other as different personalities and characters.

Zeus, King of the Gods and Ruler of Mount Olympus

As he presided over the Greek pantheon, Zeus played the role of a divine monarch with power over other deities and the whole world. He often intervened in disputes and other affairs among different gods and, of course, in the affairs of mortals. It's this role of ruler and overseer that primarily sets Zeus apart from other deities of the Greek pantheon, most of whom were also described as immensely powerful and able to profoundly affect the world.

Zeus is famously regarded as the god of thunder and the god in charge of gathering clouds. He also functioned as a father figure among the gods and a parent to many deities, including some of the twelve Olympians. This is the reason why the Olympians are usually divided into two generations, with the first generation consisting of the siblings and allies of Zeus in the Titanomachy and the second generation made up of some of the offspring of Zeus. Zeus played many other roles as well, being the maintainer of order among gods and men, giving omens, and exacting justice, all from his throne on Olympus.

According to the main narrative, peace wasn't immediately established following the war against the Titans. Instead, Gaia used the Giants to try and defeat the victorious Olympians as well. The ensuing Giant revolt, also called the Gigantomachy, was another uneven match for the Olympian gods due to the immense size and incredible power of the Giants. This was how a mortal known as Hercules came into the story after an oracle foresaw that he would help the gods defeat the Giants. Being a mortal, Hercules first needed a magic herb that would turn him invincible, the same herb that Gaia sought for her Giants. A game of wit between Zeus and Gaia followed, in which Zeus got Eos, Selene, and Helios (Dawn, Moon, and Sun, respectively) to stop shining so that he could get to the herb first. Zeus and his gods eventually won the war against the Giants, with the world enduring massive destruction in the process.

In terms of marriage, Zeus was noted as a god who had a propensity for adultery. His first marriage to Metis ended abruptly after Zeus, in a similar fashion to his predecessor, swallowed her out of fear that one of her sons would overthrow him. The marriage produced the goddess Athena, but since Zeus swallowed his wife beforehand, Athena was born to Zeus, emerging as fully grown from his head. Some of the other children of Zeus include the nine Muses, Perseus, Apollo, Artemis, Hephaestus, Ares, Hermes, Dionysus, Hercules, and numerous others.

An important and widely revered story associated with Zeus was that of the Titan Prometheus, or rather the cruel punishment that Zeus brought down upon him for his defiance. The way that Prometheus defied Zeus was by stealing fire from the gods and gifting it to mankind. For this affront, Zeus inflicted on Prometheus an eternal punishment of physical suffering, similar to how Atlas was condemned to hold up the sky forever due to his leadership of the Titans during the Titanomachy. Prometheus was sentenced to be chained to a stone so that an eagle could peck and tear at his liver for all eternity. Since Prometheus was immortal, his liver would regenerate every night, thus perpetuating an endless cycle of agony until he was rescued by Hercules.

Hera, Queen of the Gods and Goddess of

Marriage

As the wife of Zeus, Hera played the role of queen in the Greek Olympian pantheon. She was a goddess strongly associated with marriage and many things related to family life. Due to her strongly feminine role by the side of the supreme god, Hera was revered as the female ideal. In regard to marriage and family, Hera was generally the exact opposite of Zeus. She was a devoted and faithful wife to her husband, but his adultery provoked a furious jealousy and flaming hatred that Hera harbored toward the many mistresses of Zeus. Hera's jealousy was also directed at the illegitimate children that resulted from Zeus' many extramarital indiscretions. As such, the one trait that Zeus and Hera had in common was a taste for vengeance.

According to the *Theogony,* Hera and Zeus had three children together, including Ares, Hebe, and Eileithyia, the deities associated with war, youth, and childbirth, respectively. Like Zeus, Hera also had a spontaneous birth in which Hephaestus was born, which was a form of retribution on Hera's part in response to the birth of Athena. Greek mythology generally described Hephaestus, the god of metallurgy and blacksmiths, as lame. Some sources hold that he was born that way and subsequently thrown off Olympus by Zeus because of his physical disability. Other records state that his disability was the result of Hera throwing him off Olympus because she found him ugly.

One episode that perfectly encapsulates Hera's cycle of retribution toward the mistresses of Zeus and his extramarital children was her punishment of Leto, the

Titan mother of Apollo and Artemis. Once Hera learned that Leto was pregnant from Zeus, she relentlessly persecuted her and cursed any place that dared give her refuge. Leto would eventually escape to Delos, which was where Apollo was born. According to some sources, Hera also punished others preemptively and out of mere jealousy if she suspected that they might be an object of Zeus' desire. The princess Io, who was also a priestess to Hera, was thus turned into a cow. Some accounts state that it was Zeus who did this, but throughout Greek mythology, the story always revolved around Hera's endless jealous scorn.

Other stories also spoke of Hera's great vanity, notably Homer's *Iliad*. In the legendary tale, Hera had a special disdain for Paris during the Trojan War, going to great lengths to facilitate the destruction of Troy. According to Homer, her wrath stemmed primarily from the preference that Paris had for Aphrodite as the most beautiful goddess of all. As one of the key Olympian deities in Greek mythology, Hera later elicited a lot of interest from the Romans as well. In Rome's polytheistic traditions, Hera became Juno, worshipped similarly as the personification of family values and marriage but without much of the jealous wrath that Greeks attributed to Hera.

Poseidon, God of the Sea and Earthquakes

One of the most famous and referenced among the ancient Greek gods, Poseidon embodied the sea and rivers of the world. He also commanded storms, earthquakes, floods, and all manner of other natural wrath that could wreak havoc on humanity. Given his association with seas and storms, Poseidon was especially revered and feared by anyone who would embark on a maritime voyage.

Despite his ability to cause chaos and inflict great troubles upon humanity, Poseidon wasn't seen merely as a chaotic force of nation that struck at random. Rather, he was regarded as a protector to sailors and a force to be respected and pleased, lest he decide to change his demeanor. Being in Poseidon's favor was of utmost importance for any believer in ancient Greece. Additionally, Poseidon was associated with horses, particularly their taming, being regarded as the greatest horse tamer beneath the heavens. For this reason, Poseidon played a prominent role among horse breeders, an essential and potentially lucrative business venture in olden times.

In the wider context of ancient Greek mythology, the worship of Poseidon stretched back to the late Bronze Age. In Mycenaean Greece, which was at its height up to 3,500 years ago, Poseidon was likely one of the key deities that worshipers gathered around. The Mycenaean civilization was known as a seafaring one, so it's likely that Poseidon took on his maritime association a very long time ago. Classicists have also suggested that aspects of Poseidon could have been adaptations of pre-Greek traditions. In mainline Greek mythology, as a brother to Zeus and Hades, Poseidon played one of the key roles in all the divine struggles that led up to the Olympian takeover.

Ancient Greek accounts of where Poseidon resided were particularly fascinating and imaginative. He lived deep under the waves in an opulent golden palace decorated with corals and flowers. As a prolific horse tamer, Poseidon even had an undersea stable that was home to magnificent white horses near his palace. Despite his impressive dominion beneath the ocean surface, Poseidon still partook in the affairs of the land, and not always to the liking of Zeus. Indeed, some traditions spoke of a conflict between Poseidon and Zeus, in which the sea god plotted to depose the king of the gods in collusion with Hera and Athena. For this conspiracy, Poseidon received a comparatively tame punishment from Zeus, being ordered to build the mighty walls of Troy. The Romans, whose empire eventually commanded much of the Mediterranean, gave Poseidon a second life and worshiped him as Neptune.

Demeter, Goddess of Agriculture and Fertility

As a sister to Zeus, Demeter belonged to the first Olympian generation. She is also one of the oldest deities worshipped in ancient Greece, which isn't surprising given her association with agriculture and fertility. While the food production process is far removed from the average consumer nowadays, agriculture in the ancient world dominated all facets of life like few other things could. Every upset and downturn in farming yields was easily felt across the land, and despite the surplus stored in organized states, famine was widely feared. As such, agricultural deities were very common across human civilizations, worshiped and pleased with great care so as to avoid the terrifying affliction of famine.

Ancient Greece was no exception, and Demeter was looked to as a source of good fortune in farming and the guarantor of the earth's fertility. In the mythological narratives, Demeter eventually marries her brother Zeus and becomes his fourth wife. This marriage led to the birth of Persephone, famous for her subsequent abduction by Hades. Demeter was also involved with a mortal by the name of Iasion or Iasus, whom Zeus later struck down with lightning out of jealousy.

The tale of Hades' lust toward Demeter's daughter Persephone is one of the central themes of her mythology. Hades, who was Persephone's uncle, became infatuated with her from the moment he first saw her to the point where he abducted her in his chariot and drove her off to his realm in the underworld to be his wife. There have been a few different accounts regarding the abduction, with some suggesting that Zeus had given Hades permission.

Demeter eventually leveraged her authority over crops to force the other gods to help her retrieve her daughter by causing a long drought. When the mortals began to starve en masse as a result, they were no longer able to offer sacrifices to the gods. This led Zeus to intervene and order Hades to release Persephone, which he begrudgingly did. A compromise was struck, however, with an agreement that Persephone would return to the underworld to spend a part of each year with Hades.

The myth surrounding Persephone's abduction came to be strongly associated with agriculture, with some interpretations stating that the annual departure of Persephone might have symbolized the changing seasons. A few different theories have been suggested, some referring specifically to seasons and others tying the symbolism of the story to how the ancient Greeks would respond to the seasons. For instance, summers in Greece can get very hot, which is why farmers in ancient times often stored surplus grain underground to protect it from the scorching sun. Another reason why Persephone's departure to Hades might have symbolized summer is that winters in Greece aren't necessarily a time of infertility. Winter time was and still is a period during which the seeds sown in autumn would germinate and grow.

Athena, Goddess of Wisdom and Warfare

In many ways, Athena was the quintessential Greek goddess because she embodied some of the things that were of utmost importance to the ancient Greeks, such as wisdom, craftsmanship, and warfare. It's no accident that Greek mythology described Athena as Zeus' favorite daughter and attributed plenty of high virtues to her. Athena was seen as a shrewd and clever goddess who exemplified great wisdom and a courageous heart.

Athena wasn't the only ancient Greek deity associated with warfare, but she was seen as a calculating goddess with a knack for strategy, especially in regard to defensive wars. This is why, despite Athena's prowess in the affairs of war, she was often contrasted with her brother Ares, the Greek god of war. Ares was strongly connected to aggression and the love of war. Nike, the embodiment of victory in war, often had similar connotations. On the other hand, Athena was all about strength through wisdom, patience, patriotism, and strategic planning.

Athena was also described as modest and chaste, often given the epithet of "Parthenos," which signifies virginity. Unlike many other gods, Athena had no time or interest in scandalous romantic exploits and sexual indiscretions. Nonetheless, Athena was more than capable of dishing out severe punishment, born of her passion for justice. Medusa was one of the better-known victims of Athena's wrath. Once a gorgeous mortal woman, Medusa attracted the interest of Poseidon, who seduced her in one of Athena's temples. It was this sacrilegious act of disrespect that caused Athena to curse Medusa and turn her into a monster with a head of snakes instead of hair. Similarly, Athena inflicted punishments on the Achaean heroes during the Trojan War after they desecrated another one of her temples after the fall of Troy.

Hercules plays a prominent role in the story of Athena as one of her favorite heroes whom she took under her protection. Athena also had a liking for Perseus, the legendary hero who fought Medusa with the shield given to him by Athena. She also provided assistance in the epic quests of Achilles and Odysseus. Athena helped her favorite heroes in warfare but also in other ways, such as by bestowing her wisdom on them. Greek mythology sometimes credited her with some of the bright ideas that the heroes in the epics used to survive and triumph.

Athena is featured prominently in the *Iliad's* accounts of the Trojan War. As per Homer, the famous wooden horse ruse that helped the Achaeans infiltrate the impregnable walls of Troy was an idea that Odysseus got from Athena. While some deities like Hera are often difficult to distinguish from other deities in ancient artistic depictions, Athena is easily identifiable. She usually sports a golden helmet, a full set of armor, a shield, and a spear.

Apollo, God of the Sun, Music, and Prophecy

Apollo was born to Zeus and Leto as a twin to Artemis, and he became one of the most beloved and revered of all the Greek deities. Apollo also had one of the widest arrays of associations that spanned across many facets of ancient Greek life. He was worshiped as the god of music, dance, archery, divination, light, sun, truth, prophecy, healing, disease, poetry, and much more. Symbolically speaking, Apollo was closely tied to the bow, as archery was one of his central themes, along with music and divination. In many ways, Apollo was seen as the embodiment of perfection, known for his youthful beauty, radiance, power, and love of art.

Apollo and his twin sister Artemis were born on Delos amid the relentless pursuit of their mother, Leto, by enraged Hera. Hesiod wrote that Apollo was born gripping a golden sword and instantaneously reached manhood after tasting ambrosia. He soon acquired his legendary bow, which was built by Hephaestus, the greatest craftsman in the universe. Later on, Apollo was heavily involved in the Trojan War, as per the *Iliad*. Unlike Athena, Apollo was on the Trojan side, giving much help to Prince Hector, Glaucus, and Aeneas. Homer credits Apollo with preserving the lives of Trojan heroes many times and intervening on their behalf in battle. Most famously, it was Apollo who helped the Trojan prince Paris defeat and kill the invincible Achilles by piercing his heel with an arrow.

Despite all his finesse and virtues, Apollo also had a dark side, notably his ability to command pestilence and inflict other forms of divine punishment. Both Apollo and Artemis showed their capacity for cruelty when they helped their mother, Leto resolve her seemingly petty rivalry with Niobe in a rather brutal fashion. Niobe had boasted of her fertility prior to the conflict, stating that she could bear more children than Leto. In response, Leto sent her twins to kill all of Niobe's children, which included six or seven sons. This dark story is a cautionary tale about hubris and defiance toward the gods, for which Niobe paid the ultimate price.

In some stories, Apollo displayed his own divine vanity and vengefulness as well, such as his punishment of mortal Marsyas. Marsyas was a talented flute musician who made the terrible mistake of announcing that he could play better than Apollo. For this expression of hubris, Apollo had Marsyas flayed alive, after which he nailed his skin to a tree. A rather extreme conclusion to an artistic competition, the story could have also been a metaphorical tale comparing the finesse of the lyre and the primitivism of the flute, as perceived by the ancient Greeks.

Artemis, Goddess of Hunting and the Moon

Apollo's sister was a gifted archer just like him, which perfectly suited her role as the goddess of the hunt. In a wider interpretation, Artemis also embodied the wilderness and observable nature, particularly vegetation and animals. Artemis was the goddess of chastity as well, widely known for her modesty and lack of interest in the lustful affairs in which many of the other gods partook. One of her most important roles was being the goddess of childbirth and childcare. Young girls and women were under the patronage of Artemis, and she was responsible for protecting them during childbirth.

According to the writings of Callimachus around the 3rd century BC, Artemis came into her role when she was just a little girl. As the story goes, Zeus sat her on his lap when she was three years old and asked her what kind of gifts would make her happy. Among other things, Artemis asked for eternal virginity, a bow and arrow like those of Apollo, a hunting tunic, various nymphs to serve as her maids of honor, all the world's mountains, and just one city as her domain. Artemis didn't care much for cities, so she let her father choose any that he wanted since she intended to spend most of her time in the mountains.

Artemis used a silver bow built by the Cyclopes and commanded a pack of hounds on her hunts. The goddess of the hunt represented all wildlife, but wild boars and deer were especially common symbols of Artemis. Forests and the moon also evoked Artemis in ancient Greek culture, carried in the minds of many a hunter and traveler in the woodlands and those who found themselves outdoors under a moonlit night. On the side of Artemis associated with women and children, the goddess was given great importance among young brides and girls coming of age.

As the representative and protector of wildlife, it's likely that Artemis would have served as a factor of discouragement against poachers. Her disdain for the mistreatment of wildlife was exemplified in an episode during the early stages of the Trojan War. King Agamemnon incurred the wrath of Artemis by killing a deer in one of the sacred woods of Artemis. In retribution, Artemis sent unfavorable winds against the Achaean fleet as they tried to make their way to Troy. To make amends for the sacred deer, Agamemnon was forced to offer his daughter Iphigenia as a sacrifice to Artemis. Artemis took pity on the king, however, and his daughter was spared.

Ares, God of War

Ares, the Greek god of war, was a powerful and feared god. However, in spite of warfare being a fairly common occurrence in antiquity, Ares wasn't as revered as most of the other gods. More than just feared, Ares was often disliked for his fickle temper, unpredictable aggression, and overall love of war and conflict. It's perhaps no accident that the god who symbolized war was given these attributes, as this dark human phenomenon shares many of the same characteristics as Ares.

The god of war also had a rocky relationship with numerous other Olympians, particularly Poseidon, whose son Halirrhothius was killed by Ares. Another famous interaction was the seduction of Aphrodite by Ares. Apart from gods, Ares also came into conflict with Hercules, a fight in which the god drew the short end of the stick. Of all the gods, Ares was perhaps given the most human descriptions by the ancient Greeks. This wasn't reflected just in his nature but his origins, which the Greeks believed were in Thrace. This also marked Ares as something of a foreigner in the eyes of the Greeks, which could have been a deliberate choice to associate the aggressive god of conflict and disarray with foreign people.

On the bright side, Ares was portrayed as a beautiful and courageous god, and these traits were the reason Aphrodite fell for him despite her marriage to Hephaestus. The extramarital affair between Ares and Aphrodite was a source of much contention among the gods. Homer wrote that when Hephaestus caught the lovers red-handed, Ares was evicted from Olympus for a certain period.

An interesting dichotomy existed between Ares and Athena, even though they were both associated with warfare. Metaphorically speaking, Athena had a connection with all things strategic and represented the intellect needed to successfully wage war. On the other hand, Ares could be interpreted as a representative of war's chaos, brutality, unpredictability, and devastation. In the *Theogony,* Hesiod gave Ares such attributes as the sacker of cities and the piercer of shields. Befittingly, some of Ares' children included Deimos (Terror) and Phobos (Fear). However, he and Aphrodite also birthed Harmonia, the embodiment of harmony and concord. Ares lived on and became even more relevant in Roman polytheism, where he was worshipped as the god of war and called Mars. To the Romans, he was the second most important deity and was portrayed with much more virtue than among the Greeks.

Aphrodite, Goddess of Love and Beauty

Aphrodite remains one of the most famous Greek deities to this day, representing virtually everything that has to do with sexuality and passion. By extension, she was also the goddess of love and beauty. Her peculiar birth following the castration of Uranus by Cronus is another aspect of her myth that sets Aphrodite apart from other Olympians. Quite famously, Aphrodite was an unparalleled seductress, a source of endless temptation for mortals and immortals alike.

As one of the most popular deities in the Greek pantheon, Aphrodite found her way into many facets of life and society in ancient Greece, reaching well beyond her essential associations. Regular men and women both worshipped her, but so did the politicians, aristocrats, and other highborn Greeks. Across the Greek city-states, Aphrodite was a common reference in trade, politics, war, sea travel, and a number of professions, especially courtesans.

One of the most famous mythological examples of how the seductive and somewhat mischievous Aphrodite affected the realm of mortals was her role in the Trojan War. As is widely known, the war began when the Trojan prince Paris abducted Helen, a beautiful Spartan princess, and took her to Troy. Tradition states that the relationship between Paris and Helen was the result of a divine beauty contest between Hera, Athena, and Aphrodite.

In this contest, the sister of Ares and the goddess of Strife, Eris, presented a golden apple as a reward for the most beautiful among the goddesses. Zeus also played a part, appointing Paris as the judge. All three contestants offered certain enticements to Paris to win him over, and Aphrodite's offer was Helen of Sparta, the most stunning woman in existence. Less interested in the offers of invincibility and large lands to rule, as offered by the other goddesses, Paris chose Helen and thus cast his vote for Aphrodite. Unfortunately, Helen was already married to Menelaus, the king of Sparta, which is why Helen's abduction triggered the Trojan War. With the help of his brother Agamemnon, the ambitious king of Mycenae, Menelaus assembled a Greek coalition to return Helen and burn Troy to the ground.

Another famous episode was Aphrodite's involvement with the mortal Adonis, regarded as the most beautiful young man in the world. To ensure his safety, Aphrodite kept Adonis guarded by Persephone, but she, too, was unable to resist this mortal's charms and soon fell in love, refusing to return him to Aphrodite. As the two goddesses vied for control over the object of their divine lust, Zeus himself had to intervene and settle the dispute. His decision was that Adonis would spend four months every year with each of the goddesses and four months on his own. After he got killed in a hunting accident, Aphrodite turned Adonis into a flower, struck by grief.

Hephaestus, God of Blacksmiths and Craftsmanship

Hephaestus was the blacksmith for the gods and, among mortals, the god of that trade. He was also associated with fire, metallurgy, and crafts in general. Hephaestus was something of an inventor and engineer among the Olympians, responsible for keeping them supplied with their legendary weapons, armor, and various inventions. He was a builder as well, in charge of divine construction projects such as those that built extravagant homes for the gods. Being a blacksmith and smelter, Hephaestus had an obvious connection with volcanoes, and mythology held that he would set up his workshops next to them.

Apart from these important roles, Hephaestus also stuck out among the Olympians due to his lame foot and, according to some accounts, undesirable physical appearance. These characteristics are notable because it was uncommon for the ancient Greeks to describe their gods as anything less than physically flawless. They tended to be strong, healthy, and beautiful, which the Greeks never failed to depict in their artwork. Despite his physical shortcomings, Hephaestus was able to marry the seductive Aphrodite, although this wasn't necessarily her choice.

The marriage came as a result of blackmail after Hephaestus imprisoned his mother, Hera, chaining her with invisible chains. In exchange for releasing her, the blacksmith god demanded a marriage to Aphrodite. Although his demand was met, the marriage was never meant to be. After the many affairs that Aphrodite had and the conflicts that resulted from them, the two eventually divorced. Things came to a head after the aforementioned secret affair between Aphrodite and Ares, and the ensuing scandal was described rather comically in Greek mythology.

Using his signature invention of invisible chains, Hephaestus rigged his bed as a trap for the lovers and waited until they met again. The next time Aphrodite took Ares into her husband's bed, the two were bound and left at the mercy of Hephaestus. His punishment was to summon all the other gods to behold their shame, subjecting them to ridicule. Aphrodite and Ares were soon released, however, but they both had to flee for a while.

According to some texts, Hephaestus was also noted as the father of Erechtheus, the legendary first ruler of Athens. From the 4th century BC onward, a distinction was made between Erechtheus and Erichthonius, leading to uncertainty as to who the actual first legendary ruler of Athens was. Nonetheless, the writings of Euripides suggest that the Athenians referred to themselves as the *Erechtheidai,* which translates as "the sons of Erechtheus." Homer wrote that Erechtheus was raised by Athena after being conceived from the semen of Hephaestus, which fell to the earth after he unsuccessfully tried to assault Athena.

This is why Erechtheus was described as having been "earth-born." Some traditions also state that the Athenians themselves were born of this same incident.

Hermes, Messenger of the Gods and Guide of Souls to the Underworld

Mischief and intelligence were some of the defining characteristics of Hermes. As a messenger for the gods, Hermes played a very special role among the Olympians. He was seen and worshiped as a connecting thread or bridge between humanity and the gods. This unique position resulted in Hermes taking on a very wide and versatile array of associations. Those who hoped for wealth, particularly traders, had a special reverence for Hermes as he was associated with luck and good favor with the gods. He was also the god of animal husbandry, travel, sleep, language, fertility, and much more.

The mischievous side of Hermes, coupled with his connection to luck, made him very popular among some of the shadier characters in society, particularly thieves and gamblers. Indeed, Hermes was regarded as the inventor of dice. He also demonstrated his versatility in his inventions, as the ancient Greeks believed that he invented the lyre and the Greek alphabet. Folks in the business of raising sheep, which was a very important vocation, revered Hermes as their divine patron. Perhaps another reason why Hermes was so versatile was his long history. Like Poseidon, Hermes dates back to early Mycenae.

Traditions state that he was born to Zeus and Maia, who was a nymph and the daughter of Atlas. Hermes' mischievous nature didn't result from malice but was the feature of his unquenchable thirst for entertainment. Hermes exhibited such traits even as a baby, proving himself a capable thief when he stole a whole herd of cattle from Apollo, who was his half-brother. As usual, he did this for his own amusement, altering the cattle's hoofs to make their tracks point in the opposite direction, thus confusing anyone who'd try to follow them. When he was eventually found out, Zeus demanded that Hermes compensate Apollo for his sacred cattle by giving him his lyre, which became a famous feature of Apollo's mythology. Hermes also sometimes stole the legendary weapons and other prized possessions of gods like Poseidon, Artemis, and Aphrodite.

As entertaining as the anecdotes of Hermes' tomfoolery were, it was still his role as the divine messenger that really made him a household name. It's the reason why Hermes secured a prominent place in so many stories that the ancient Greeks wrote and told about their gods. Hermes primarily carried messages for Zeus, but he also fulfilled more demanding tasks involving battles against monsters like Argos and some of the Giants. He also came to be associated with the dead because another one of his main jobs required him to lead souls to the river Styx in the underworld. In the famous myth, souls would arrive at the Styx and be placed on Charon's boat, which would then take them to Hades.

Dionysus, God of Wine, Celebration, and Ecstasy

The meaning of Dionysus to the ancient Greeks is difficult to summarize briefly, but if it had to be done in a word, the word could be joy. Still, no singular word can do justice to the incredibly wide range of things that Dionysus symbolized and embodied. Theater, celebration, and wine were the main associations, but others included fruit, plants, festivities, ecstasy amid rituals, religious fervor, fertility, insanity, and more. In regard to wine, Dionysus wasn't merely a symbol of the alcoholic beverage but also a patron and god of wine-makers, a profession held in high regard back then as it is nowadays.

Zeus was the father of Dionysus, but traditions vary significantly regarding the identity of his mother and the manner of his conception, birth, and upbringing. A common interpretation holds that he was born to Zeus as a result of his affair with the mortal Semele. Like other mistresses of Zeus, Semele thus attracted the wrath of Hera's jealousy. Preferring not to strike her dead directly, Hera devised an insidious plan. She convinced Semele to ask Zeus to fully reveal his divine body to her, knowing that such a sight would be lethal to any mortal.

Semele was still pregnant when this happened, and although she died immediately, Zeus plucked the unborn Dionysus from the clutches of death. Zeus then kept him in his thigh until he was strong enough to survive, after which he entrusted his care to Silenus, a forest god associated with drunkenness and wine. Silenus thus became a foster father to Dionysus and raised him as a child with the help of his satyrs, the male spirits of nature in Greek mythology.

Both Homer and Hesiod closely associated Dionysus with joy and cheerfulness, with Homer specifically referring to him as the "joy of men." While Dionysus himself would have likely acquired his interest in wine-making from his father, Greek mythology credits this god as the one who taught this important trade to mankind. The association of Dionysus with theater might have come from the frenzied rituals that worshipers organized in his honor. These rituals were essentially celebrations on an extreme level, involving uncontrollable dancing that led the participants to a state of transcendence. This might have been how Greek theater came to be since the transcendental nature of the festive frenzy was akin to the way in which theatrical actors transcended their own identities in favor of the characters they were playing.

Chapter 3: Legendary Heroes

Apart from the seemingly countless deities, creatures, and monsters, another key aspect of Greek mythology revolves around various legendary heroes and their epic adventures. Some of these stories might have been inspired by historical events and characters, but they are largely mythologized and often serve to tell extensive stories about people, gods, and life. The heroes of Greek mythology have been widely explored in the literature of ancient Greece and continue to be analyzed to this day. The ancient Greek writings that chronicle the lives of these mythical, semi-divine giants among men also comprise some of the oldest preserved literature that represents an invaluable gem of overall human cultural heritage.

Perseus and the Gorgon Medusa

In Greek mythology, there were generations of legendary heroes, which helped maintain a degree of chronology in the retellings of their epic feats. It also provided for a perception of historicity and allowed the Greeks to put these old tales in perspective and context among one another. From the perspective of the historiography that studies antiquity, it's also possible to establish a certain chronological order of when these myths emerged and which of the heroes came before others. The story of Perseus is among the oldest of the legendary heroes of Greek mythology. It stretched across time but also space, reaching virtually all the Greek polities and becoming a truly Pan-Hellenic legend.

Greek mythology seems to have maintained an awareness of how historically old the legend of Perseus and Medusa was. This follows from the fact that traditional chronology places the life and adventures of Perseus three generations prior to those of Hercules. The narrative of how Perseus was born is told in a manner that presents a regular, mortal origin with a side of intrigue that involves divine intervention and extramarital indiscretion. Namely, Perseus had two mortal parents, Danaos and Danae. His mother, Danae, was the daughter of Acrisius, the ruler of the ancient kingdom of Argos, located north of Sparta on the Peloponnese peninsula.

At one point, Danae was imprisoned by her father because of a dark prophecy given to him by an oracle, predicting that one of his grandsons would kill him. Out of fear, Acrisius had his daughter confined to a tower made of bronze close to his palace so as to ensure she would bear no sons. Some retellings state that Danae's cell was underground, but in either case, she was beyond the reach of any mortal. Danae had attracted the interest of Zeus, however, and no human prison could keep him out. Zeus transformed himself into a golden rain so that he could rain down into Danae's prison, impregnating her upon contact. Acrisius eventually found out that Danae had given birth and, skeptical of her explanations, enclosed her and the boy in a wooden chest, which he threw into the sea. Adrift among the waves, their safety was ensured by Zeus who intervened by asking Poseidon to see them safely to the island of Seriphos. A fisherman by the name of Diktys found Danae and her son washed up on the shore, so young

Perseus would make his home on the island until he grew up into a strong young man.

The simplified version of Medusa's origins as a Gorgon is the aforementioned vengeance of Athena for what she perceived as Medusa's desecration of her temple with Poseidon. However, the more detailed mythology behind Medusa is a tragic story of a mortal woman's unfair fate at the hands of the gods. While she was accused of seducing Poseidon and thus offending her goddess Athena, it was actually the infatuated and lustful sea god that raped Medusa in Athena's temple. Unable to inflict her vengeance on another god, Athena instead punishes Medusa by turning her into a terrible Gorgon monster.

There is also an element of jealousy that crops up in some of the myths, as Medusa was known to be a beautiful young maiden. Another version of the myth focuses on this jealousy and is equally cruel to Medusa. In that story, Medusa asked her goddess to allow her to travel south so that she could lay her eyes on the sun for the first time after spending her life in the sunless far north. Athena rejected Medusa's request, which frustrated Medusa, and said it was the result of Athena's jealousy over her great mortal beauty. This boastful affront infuriated Athena, who then turned Medusa into a Gorgon. She thus became a terrifying creature with claws, wings, and snakes slithering from her head where her hair used to flow, cursed to turn any man she glanced at into stone.

Medusa was one of three Gorgons, who also included her sisters Stheno and Euryale. All three sisters were born to Gaia, with Medusa as the mortal of the three, and their home was in a mystical land of grass and flowers beyond the ocean's horizon. When Athena inflicted her cruel retribution on Medusa, the attempt by her sisters to help her resulted in them meeting the same fate, which is how the three Gorgons came to be. They were soon exiled from their homeland and forced to find a new place in the south, where they were condemned to suffer in solitude while often being targeted by monster-slaying heroes in pursuit of glory.

None of the challengers could match Medusa's terrible powers until Perseus came along. The showdown between Medusa and Perseus was the result of a challenge by King Polydectes, the ruler of the island of Seriphos and brother to the fisherman Diktys. The island king had become infatuated with Danae and sought to take her hand, but Perseus was an insurmountable obstacle to his designs. Upon hearing the powerful young hero boasting that he could slay the infamous Gorgon monster Medusa, the king saw an opportunity to get rid of him. During a feast in the company of other heroes, Polydectes publically challenged Perseus to journey into Medusa's dominion and bring back her head.

The chances that Perseus would prevail where many others had fallen were slim, but neither Perseus nor King Polydectes expected that the gods would cast their favor upon Perseus. Athena and Hermes were the first to offer their aid, instructing Perseus to seek counsel from the three Graeae, who were witch-like siblings of the Gorgons. Perseus had to strong-arm the witches somewhat, but they eventually gave him important insights that would help bring Medusa down. Hermes armed Perseus with a mighty sword that could decapitate Medusa, while Athena gave him a highly polished, legendary shield. The information extracted from the Graeae helped Perseus locate other important items, including a pair of winged sandals and a cap of Hades, which granted him invisibility. The last essential piece of equipment was an enchanted bag, specifically designed to carry the Gorgon's head and protect the carrier from her deadly gaze.

Perseus then used his sandals to soar across the sky toward the edge of the earth, where he found the Gorgons. Thanks to the stunning polish of Athena's shield, Perseus was able to use it as a mirror to look at the Gorgons without being turned to stone. With his legendary sword and cap of invisibility, Perseus was able to make quick work of Medusa's head, easily sneaking up to her and dealing the lethal blow. The winged horse Pegasus emerged from her neck as the Gorgon's head fell from her shoulders. Perseus quickly but carefully placed the head in his magical bag and mounted the winged horse, vacating the area before the other Gorgons could catch him.

Some traditions also chronicle the hero's triumphant journey home to Seriphos, during which he met and fell in love with Andromeda. Using the head of Medusa as a weapon to turn his enemies to stone, Perseus overcame challengers to his union with Andromeda and eventually made his way home. In some versions, Perseus returns to the island to find that his mother had been mistreated by the king, prompting him to present the Gorgon trophy in a way that quickly turns the king into stone.

Theseus and the Minotaur

Theseus was a prolific fighter at whose feet fell many a monster and villain. He eventually became one of the most famous legendary Greek heroes, but he was particularly important to the Athenians, who treated him as a symbol of the perfection that all mortals should aspire toward. In Greek traditions, Theseus was also believed to have been one of the earliest kings of Athens. In his legendary adventures, Theseus battled the Amazons, centaurs, the infamous Minotaur in his labyrinth, and many other opponents. The Athenians saw Theseus as a just and courageous individual while also associating him with their system of democracy. His various battles, especially the slaying of the Minotaur, were immortalized in many forms of Greek art, including Greek tragic plays, vase paintings, and literature.

The adventures of Theseus began when he was a very young man, notably during his Six Labors, also known as the six entrances to the underworld. These adventures happened while Theseus was making his epic return to Athens to claim the throne that was rightfully his. Theseus had a claim because his father was Aegeus, the king of Athens, who was married to Aethra. According to one version, Aegeus didn't want his son to know who his father was until he came of age, instructing Aethra to take the baby to her father, Pittheus, who ruled Troezen in northeastern Peloponnese. This was where Theseus grew up, with many believing that he was actually a son of Poseidon, as reflected in certain traditions.

To make his way back to Athens once he grew up, Theseus retrieved the hidden sword of his father and set out on a dangerous journey, battling many monsters and enemies along the way. By the time he made his way to Athens, Theseus had left a string of dead, villainous monsters in his wake. Many of these monsters and bandits, such as Periphetes, Sinis, Sciron, Cercyon, and others, shared a common theme: that they were disruptive and aggressive toward travelers who wandered into their territory.

The most famous legendary showdown of Theseus by far was with the Minotaur. In what could have been a metaphor for troublesome interstate relations, the story of the Minotaur involved an obligation of Athens to send regular shipments of seven men and seven women to feed the Minotaur. One of the most unsettling monsters of Greek mythology by far, the Minotaur featured a bull's head atop a man's body. It belonged to the Cretan king Minos, who kept the monster in a labyrinth at Knossos. Theseus was determined to free Athens of this terrible tribute in blood forever by personally killing the monster.

He infiltrated the labyrinth by signing up as one of the young men in the next shipment to Crete. Theseus thus entered the labyrinth, itself a terrifying invention famous for its confusing turns and dead ends, constructed to disorient the victims condemned to being stalked, hunted down, and devoured by the Minotaur. Minos' daughter Ariadne helped the hero as he navigated the labyrinth by using a long string to mark his path for the journey back.

Upon finding the Minotaur, Theseus made quick work of slaying the beast and then followed the string back to leave the labyrinth.

Unfortunately, his return to Athens was unceremoniously tragic. As he approached the homeland, Theseus forgot to change his black sail to white, which was agreed as a way of signaling to his father that he was safe and victorious. Upon seeing the black sail, Aegeus assumed the worst and gave in to his grief, jumping off a cliff to his death. The sea that took him would be known as the Aegean from that mythical moment to this very day.

Hercules and His Twelve Labors

Known to the ancient Greeks as Heracles, Hercules got his now-popular name from the Romans, who revered his myth just as much, if not more, than the Greeks. This is perhaps the reason why the Roman name eventually came to dominate his memory across the West and remains as such to this day. Half-brother to Perseus through their father Zeus, Hercules was a major figure in Greek myth and legend, serving as the epitome of strength, endurance, and heroism. He was seen as a divine figure even though he was born as a mortal. Through his extraordinary feats, specifically the twelve labors, Hercules was able to attain immortality and earn his place among the gods. As the champion of the Olympians, Hercules was often considered the greatest human hero of all time.

The mortal, paternal side of Hercules' family came from Mycenae, with both of his parents originating from Argos. Due to a string of unfortunate events and quarrels with the king, Hercules' father, Amphitryon had to take his wife Alcmene and flee to Thebes before Hercules was born. Traditions state that Amphitryon was actually a stepfather to Hercules, as he was conceived in an extramarital relationship between Alcmene and Zeus. In the usual Greek fashion, this divine parentage offers an explanation for the legendary strength of Hercules. A particularly famous episode from the childhood of Hercules happened when jealous Hera, enraged by her husband's affair as usual, sent two snakes to kill Hercules in his infancy. The snakes were no match for Hercules, even though he was just a baby, so he strangled them. Hera's wrath aside, most other Olympians had a liking for Hercules, especially Athena.

One of the centerpieces of the myth of Hercules consisted of his twelve labors, which came to pass as a result of Hera's vicious persecution of Hercules. After Hercules married his wife Megara, who was the daughter of the king of Thebes, they had five children. Unwilling to allow a bastard of Zeus to live a fulfilling life, Hera casts a spell of insanity on Hercules, which drives him to murder his entire family. After regaining sanity, Hercules was devastated by what he had done, turning to Apollo for guidance. The advice attained through an oracle at Delphi was for Hercules to achieve redemption by serving his cousin and king, Eurystheus. Eurystheus became the king of Mycenae, Tiryns, and Argos after Hera deliberately delayed the birth of Hercules so that Eurystheus would be born first and thus become the ruler instead of Hercules.

When it came time for Hercules to begin his service, Hera intervened against Hercules once again by instructing his cousin to send Hercules on suicide missions against invincible opponents, and so the twelve labors of Hercules commenced. As described in Pseudo-Apollodorus' Bibliotheca, the first assignment was to slay the Nemean Lion. This enchanted beast had tormented the inhabitants of Nemea for a while by that point, most likely as a divine punishment. The lion was protected by an impenetrable hide that could not be pierced with any weapon. In an epic form of improvisation, Hercules used his bare hands to strangle the monster instead.

The second mission revolved around the legend of the Lernaean Hydra, a ferocious monster that could breathe fire from more than one serpent head. The monster's regenerative superpowers are especially famous, allowing two new heads to grow from the neck whenever one head is cut off. The Hydra lived in a swampy area close to Lerna, where it was sent by Hera to harass and destroy the hero's hometown. With the help of his nephew Iolaus, who used fire to prevent Hydra's stumps from growing new heads, Hercules finally prevailed.

The third labor required Hercules to capture one of the sacred deer of Artemis, known as the Ceryneian or Golden Hind of Artemis. Artemis initially wanted to intervene, but when Hercules described his mission, she sanctioned his capture of the hind, allowing him to bring it back alive. The fourth labor was another hunt for a live animal, referred to as the Erymanthian Boar, a loose wild boar wreaking havoc. Once again, the hero succeeded and brought the animal back to Mycenae. The main difficulty in the third and fourth labors was that they were time-consuming, which is why they carry a connotation of virtuous patience.

For his fifth labor, Hercules had to get his hands dirty in a literal sense, as his job was to clean the stables that housed what might have been the largest animal herd in history. The stables belonged to Augeas, the king of Elis, and they numbered around 3,000 animals that produced poisonous feces. The dung piles were so enormous and so toxic that they threatened the entire city, and Hercules had to clean it all up in a day. The task was no match for Hercules, and he was able to dig two massive ditches near the stables, shoveling all the excrement into them. By diverting the rivers Pineios and Alpheios, Hercules washed the ditches in one of the most ecologically unsound waste disposal efforts in history.

The sixth, seventh, and eighth labors involved additional tasks of killing or capturing problematic beasts. The kill list included the disruptively aggressive Stymphalian Birds and the rampaging Cretan Bull, while the man-eating Mares of Diomedes had to be brought back alive. The Cretan Bull, which terrorized the citizens of Knossos, might have been the beast that mated with Pasiphae, which gave birth to the dreaded Minotaur. There are also versions of the myth that describe the Cretan Bull mission as a task to capture the bull.

Job nine required Hercules to steal Hippolyta's girdle. Hippolyta was queen to the fearsome female warriors known as the Amazons, which made it a dangerous mission. The value of the girdle was in the fact that it came from Ares. Hercules and his helpers tried to infiltrate the

Amazon homeland near the Black Sea, but Hera had already set the Amazons into combat mode to stop Hercules. Nonetheless, the mission was a success, with Hercules bringing the girdle to Eurystheus. The tenth labor was yet another capture mission, which involved the stealing of a cattle herd belonging to Geryon, a monstrous giant living on the island of Erytheia. The herd was also guarded by the horrific Orthrus, a two-headed dog with the tail of a snake, and Erytion, a herdsman born to Ares. Using his mighty club and poisoned arrows dipped in Hydra's blood, Hercules inevitably prevailed.

The eleventh labor of Hercules was particularly significant because it was intertwined with some other major Greek myths and was an affront to Hera herself. The job was to steal the golden apples belonging to the nymphs called Hesperides and protected by Hera. Instructed by the goddess, a dragon with a hundred heads called Ladon was the guardian of the sacred apples. Hercules also had to find out where the fruits were, so he first set out on an investigation.

Along the way, he ran into Prometheus, chained to a rock by Zeus. After Hercules set the cursed Titan free and killed the eagle tormenting him, Prometheus told him to ask his brother Atlas about the whereabouts of the golden apples. Atlas, also enduring his punishment by Zeus, agreed to help in return for Hercules holding up the sky instead of him for a while. Atlas then tried to trick Hercules by leaving him to hold the heavens forever, but he failed, and the hero went on to complete his mission.

By the twelfth labor, Eurystheus was in disbelief at the persistently triumphant Hercules, and so he decided to give him a task that he knew was impossible. As his last mission on the path toward atonement, Hercules was ordered to go down to Hades and capture Cerberus, the infamous three-headed canine monstrosity standing at the gates of the underworld. Not content to let his physical might outshine his wit, Hercules took a diplomatic approach and convinced Hades to hand over the beast on the condition that he capture it without using weapons. Hades agreed, and Hercules then brought Cerberus back to Mycenae. Eurystheus cowered in fear at the sight of Hercules bringing Cerberus in.

Achilles

Another one of the widely famous Greek heroes, Achilles, has entered the collective human consciousness in the same way as Hercules. As a key character in the frequently referenced *Iliad,* Achilles is certainly one of the most famous heroic figures in all of written history, but he's also a powerful symbol. For the ancient Greeks, Achilles was the most proficient warrior humanity had ever produced. Because of his unmatched skill in battle, Achilles attained a legend of invincibility despite the fact that his story ended with his death. In its own way, the tale of Achilles is also a tale of immortalization, but whereas Hercules became physically immortal by joining the gods, Achilles did so via the endurance of his name and glory.

While an image of perfection in his physical presence and art of combat, Achilles had a number of character flaws, namely his ill temper and persistent wrath. He was the child of the Nereid (sea nymph) Thetis and Peleus, himself a legendary hero and king of Phthia. When Achilles was a baby, his mother attempted to make him immortal. Some traditions state that Thetis did this by holding her son over a godly fire, while other versions explain that she dipped him into the underworld river Styx. In either case, she held the boy by his heel, leaving it as the only vulnerable part of his body and, quite famously, causing his eventual downfall at the hands of the Trojan prince Paris. Achilles was raised in secrecy on Skyros and most likely tutored by the wise Chiron, a centaur who was also responsible for the early education of Hercules.

Greek mythology mostly focuses on the Trojan War when narrating the life and glory of Achilles, but these traditions also state that he was initially reluctant to join the Greek campaign. It was Odysseus who managed to talk the mighty warrior into it, enticing him with promises of eternal glory in a war that would never be forgotten. Achilles thus gathered 50 ships and boarded with his army of Myrmidons, all legendary warriors that Zeus himself had made from ants.

Throughout the grueling ten-year siege of Troy, Achilles was unstoppable in battle, laying waste to the enemy and their settlements. Despite the battlefield successes, his vanity, temper, and propensity for conflict were a persistent hindrance to the Greek war effort. An important turning point, as explained in the *Iliad,* which will be explored in greater detail in the next chapter, was the falling out that Achilles had with the Mycenaean king Agamemnon. The personal conflict between Achilles and the leader of the Greek army partly resulted from their quarrel over Briseis and Chryseis, two beautiful women captured by Achilles.

Achilles took a liking to Briseis and refused to hand her over to Agamemnon, offering him Chryseis instead. When Agamemnon rejected her father's generous ransom, the protector of Troy, Apollo was enraged even worse than before since Chryseis was one of his priestesses. To force Agamemnon to release the priestess, Apollo brought down a devastating plague on the Greek forces, forcing the king to yield to the will of Apollo. Now left without his spoils, Agamemnon kidnapped Briseis from Achilles, prompting the mighty warrior and his Myrmidons to boycott the war.

Achilles eventually agreed to let his army fight a defensive war without him, but this resulted in the death of his cherished lifetime friend Patroclus, slain by the sword of the Trojan prince Hector. News of his death sent Achilles into a fit of seething rage and hatred, much to the joy of Agamemnon. With Achilles back in action, the Greeks were able to turn the tide of the war, and not even Apollo himself could protect Prince Hector from the murderous wrath of Achilles.

Odysseus

Odysseus, the king of Ithaca, is most famous for his key roles in Homer's *Iliad* and *Odyssey*, but he was a major legendary figure in many epic tales and traditions across the Greek world. He is less commonly known under the Latin Roman variation of his name, Ulysses. Odysseus and the stories about him have entrenched themselves in literature and culture across the world, especially in the West. Similarly to Hercules, the fame and immense legacy of Odysseus and his depictions in Homer are apparent in modern language. Whereas the adjective "herculean" signifies a tremendously challenging undertaking or great power and strength, the word "odyssey" denotes a long, arduous voyage that involves many challenges and twists of fate.

In Greek mythology, the Ithacan king was described as an industrious individual of great wit, courage, charisma, and leadership. In Homer's writing, he was one of the decisive actors in ensuring a Greek victory in the Trojan War. Odysseus was described as a master strategist who used creativity to outwit the enemy. The legendary Trojan horse, perhaps the most famous tale of a military ruse in history, was the brainchild of Odysseus. This big wooden figure that he built was the turning point in the war, as it allowed the Greeks to hide a number of troops inside and infiltrate the impenetrable fortress of Troy. Apart from his ingenuity, Odysseus was also an eloquent and inspirational speaker who knew his way around the human mind, often capable of swaying others to his point of view. In the *Iliad,* Odysseus helps the Greeks win the war, while the *Odyssey* chronicles his long and difficult journey back to his kingdom of Ithaca.

As per the traditional narratives, there are some discrepancies regarding the familial origins of Odysseus. As king of Ithaca, he led the Cephallenians, inhabitants of the largest Ionian island known today as Cephalonia. According to Homer, he was born to Laertes, the earlier king of the Cephallenians, and Anticlea, the king's wife and queen of Ithaca. Other sources, however, spoke about Odysseus as the great-grandson of Hermes or the son of Sisyphus. The latter tradition explains that Odysseus was actually bought by Laertes from Sisyphus. Whatever the origins of Odysseus were, he also had a family of his own after marrying Penelope, who bore him a son named Telemachus. Odysseus had a number of other children as well.

As one of the most revered heroes of ancient Greek legends, Odysseus was a favorite of Athena. Like most heroes, he was given a number of divine attributes in the stories, which tended to focus on his famous intelligence. In fact, Homer wrote that the mental faculties of Odysseus could match those of Zeus. Naturally, Odysseus was also a great fighter who could take on virtually all comers, although the title of the greatest Greek warrior in the *Iliad* undoubtedly belonged to Achilles. Owed to his fighting skills but especially the fact that he helped conquer and destroy Troy, for which Homer crowned him the "sacker of cities."

Among the many epic stories of Odysseus, the voyage to Ithaca after the Trojan War is perhaps the most famous. This difficult, ten-year journey across the unruly seas was in great part a consequence of divine wrath toward the Greeks. Due to their cruelty toward the defeated Trojans, the grotesque destruction of the city, and the desecration of temples, the Greek fleet incurred the fury of a number of gods. Because of this, the Greek victory over Troy would be a pyrrhic one, with most of their fleet being struck down by disaster on the way home. In an epic display of perseverance and resilience, Odysseus became one of very few survivors by the end of the ordeal.

The voyage home involved many stops, turns, detours, challenges, and perils. Odysseus found himself having various run-ins with the gods, sometimes friendly and sometimes not. More often than not, Odysseus was met with hostility by the various characters and creatures he encountered, including Cyclopes, giants, deities, and sorcerers. The hero had to fight or evade such challengers, usually by outwitting them in some way. It was also a journey filled with temptations, such as the one encountered when Odysseus and his men met the so-called Lotus Eaters. The plants they ate would enable the consumer to forget about their homeland, which could have perhaps enticed a weaker man when faced with a seemingly impossible journey of ever-dwindling odds. However, Odysseus stayed firm and never once considered giving up, pressing on despite all hardships, as the next chapter will describe in more detail.

Chapter 4: Epic Tales

While the title of the oldest preserved piece of human literature is usually given to the Mesopotamian *Epic of Gilgamesh,* the ancient Greeks also left a monumental early mark with their epic stories and poems. As mentioned earlier, these epics were initially passed down as oral traditions, but they really came into their own with the writings of Homer and subsequent Greek poets and dramatists. Ancient Greek classics have enabled the old Greek civilization to affect the literature and art of the world in ways that few other cultures have accomplished.

Stories about the Argonauts and the epic tales found in the *Iliad* and the *Odyssey* are also important sources in the study of Greek mythology. These stories are complex narratives with many characters, and they often revolve around legendary Greek heroes, their exploits, and their interactions with the gods. Understanding the mythology around these legendary figures, as covered in this book thus far, is important when learning the basics of Greek mythology. However, studying the history, contents, and themes of the literary classics is equally essential in grasping the culture and mentality that have given birth to these timeless myths.

The Iliad: Trojan War and the Wrath of Achilles

Unlike some of the adaptations of the *Iliad,* this epic poem doesn't chronicle the entirety of the mythical Trojan War and instead focuses just on one part of it, ending before the final conclusion of the war. The narrative consists mostly of the closing year of the war, describing how a coalition of Greek city-states, which Homer referred to collectively as the Achaeans, defeated the Trojans. Despite all its references to great heroes, valor in battle, and glory, the *Iliad* pulls no punches in portraying the brutal reality of war as well. In fact, the lack of gallantry that some of the Greeks in the story show toward the Trojans is an important theme in the poem.

The *Iliad* explores many aspects of human nature, relationships, motivations, and mentality through the lens of warfare. Homer uses war as the ultimate setting that brings unfiltered human nature to the forefront in a way that few other circumstances can accomplish, highlighting the flaws and virtues of the story's characters on full display. Pride plays a prominent role, particularly in the motives of those who had initiated the Trojan War, but also in the subsequent interactions between the main actors. Rage or wrath is another centerpiece, mostly embodied by the mighty Achilles. Throughout the *Iliad,* the invisible yet omnipresent hand of fate hovers over all human affairs and the many toils and struggles of the main characters. As such, the *Iliad* features an overarching theme of destiny and the inability of any man to escape it.

In terms of structure, the *Iliad* consists of 24 books, totaling 15,693 lines written in dactylic hexameter, a common scheme in ancient Greek poetry. Since the original was put together in the 8th century BC, the *Iliad*, like many other pieces of ancient literature, has been published many times in various versions. The epic poem's first English publication went out in the late 16th century in its most established English version. Along with the *Odyssey,* the *Iliad* is considered a jewel of Greek literature, and this isn't a recent perception. Homer enjoyed a legendary status among the ancient Greeks themselves, many of whom considered him the greatest author to have ever lived.

Indeed, Homer was so famous and revered across ancient Greece that he was often referred to just as "the poet." In the many centuries since then, the *Iliad* has met similar acclaim across the world not simply for its age and historical importance but also for the merits of its actual story. There are very few other pieces of literature that can boast to be as old and yet as widely read and enjoyed by common audiences to this very day. Whenever the works of Homer are mentioned, the chances are good that everyone in the room has either read his epics or has heard about them. Many other important bits of writing from antiquity have been preserved, yet the *Iliad* and the *Odyssey* are almost unique in their ability to captivate and engage a modern audience, making these classics truly timeless.

The conflict between Agamemnon and Achilles is one of the key plot points in the poem, and the story begins with Achilles sitting on the sidelines of the war due to a grudge. It is an epic clash of hot tempers and big egos that keeps getting worse as the *Iliad* progresses until it's eventually overshadowed by a much greater conflict that sends Achilles over the edge. As discussed in the previous chapter, the indomitable Achilles begins to unwind in a very destructive way after the death of his friend Patroclus.

This incident and its consequences are a major part of the plot and a key moment that determines the war's outcome and the fates of many characters. The fact that "the rage of Achilles" is something of an unofficial subtitle to the poem highlights the emotional weight of Patroclus' death and Achilles' reaction to it, particularly the horrific vengeance he would inflict on Hector.

Coming out of his grudged stupor and boycott of Agamemnon's war, Achilles made a request to his mother for a new set of armor built by the god Hephaestus himself. Homer described it as the most stunning armor in history, featuring immense strength and astonishing the onlookers with its splendor, decorations, and shine. Dressed in his new armor and seething with homicidal rage, Achilles took to battle, leading his troops against the Trojans with renewed zeal. A string of crushing blows against the Trojans ensued, littering the land with the corpses of many brave warriors. Apollo, the protector of Troy, tried his best to protect Prince Hector, but to no avail. The final showdown came in the form of a duel between Achilles and Hector right outside the impenetrable Trojan walls.

Hector was also a courageous man and a great warrior, perhaps the greatest son of Troy. The prince tried to evade and survive as well as he could, but the mighty Achilles was relentless. Before long, Hector fell to the ground, but his death was merely an overture of suffering for him and his family. Not content to just slay the killer of Patroclus, Achilles tied Hector to his chariot and dragged him across the rough Trojan soil right before his family's very eyes. Desecrating the body of his fallen enemy and denying him a proper funeral by dragging him back to camp, Achilles, blind with rage, had committed the worst sacrilege against the conventions of war and honor. With Achilles back in the fight and heroic Hector slain, Troy's fate was surely sealed.

The entire story is a chain of events conditioned by cause and effect, especially through seemingly random twists of fate. Homer often personifies fate by describing how the gods make their choices and influence events, but even the gods often leave things to chance. For instance, in the showdown between Achilles and Hector, Zeus weighed the odds for both heroes with the so-called golden scales of fate. The divine contraption swayed in Achille's favor, and that's all it took for Achilles to catch up to Hector and end his life with a spear to the throat.

The entire ordeal, along with the fall of Troy as a result, can be tied to Achilles' fateful decision to allow Patroclus to lead the Myrmidons into battle while wearing the hero's armor. Achilles tried to be cautious, ordering Patroclus to only fight defensively and not pursue the Trojans even if the tide of battle turned in favor of the Greeks. However, when Patroclus charged into battle wearing the armor of Achilles, the Trojans were horrified at the sight of the invincible warrior coming after them, causing a rout. Drunk with success and glory, Patroclus pressed on after the Trojans and got himself killed.

In Homer, Greek heroes are humanized and reflective, often engaging in deep introspection. The likes of Hector are described as family men filled with love for their country and their families, equally loved in return by their wives and their parents. The gruesome treatment of Hector's corpse by Achilles in view of his family, wife Andromache, and his father, King Priam, is thus given tremendous weight. Hector himself is introspective and worried following his killing of Patroclus, as he dreads his own inevitable doom and that of his country, knowing that Achilles will return with a vengeance.

The prince's one-on-one encounter with Achilles was, in a way, Hector's desperate attempt to offer his life in payment, with a slim hope that it would give satisfaction to the unstoppable Achilles and spare his country and people. Even Achilles, with all his ferocity and bloodlust, is still very human. Homer doesn't shy away from portraying the mightiest warrior to have ever lived in moments of weakness, such as when Achilles cries to his mother following his troubles with Agamemnon.

The chariot incident wouldn't be the first time that uncontrollable Achilles would irritate the gods, but his cruel and undignified conduct toward Hector particularly enraged the immortals. The *Illiad's* final book is especially emotional as it revolves around King Priam sneaking into the Greek camp to plead with Achilles to return his son's body so that it could be washed and given all due rites. Hermes helped Priam find his way, and Athena granted him wisdom to appeal to Achilles. King Priam then stated his case in a compelling speech, which moved the cold heart of Achilles to grant his request. This is where the *Iliad* ends, but the war's final phase and the continued warpath of Achilles until his eventual death by Prince Paris continue in other stories.

The honorable Prince Hector and his demise have sometimes been interpreted as metaphors for the city of Troy and its tragic fate. The entire story of the *Iliad* is filled to the brim with such metaphors, although it's not entirely allegorical. The poem starts with the wrath of Achilles, and his last act in combat, at least in the poem, is an act of rage. Still, the very end of the poem features a certain thaw when Achilles permits Priam to take Hector's body. Even though the terrible destruction of Troy is an eventual inevitability, the *Iliad* chooses to end in a moment of understanding and empathy between two men struck by grief and loss.

The Odyssey: The Adventures and Homecoming of Odysseus

As briefly mentioned earlier, the *Odyssey* focuses on the long aftermath of the Trojan War through the eyes of Odysseus. However, this epic poem is more than an entertaining story chronicling an epic quest. Instead, it abounds in meaning, philosophy, reflection, and a number of important themes, just like Homer's other legendary piece. Since Odysseus is an important character in the *Iliad,* the *Odyssey* can also be seen as a follow-up or sequel to the other poem. Odysseus the Cunning, as he was sometimes characterized in the epics, was a beloved character in Greek mythology due to his lovable personality and cleverness. The ten years in the *Odyssey* are a string of adventures and tricky situations that Odysseus lands in and overcomes thanks to these qualities but also his courage.

Not only does Odysseus have to contend with stormy seas, monsters, and other enemies, but he also encounters temptation in the form of women enticing him to betray his wife, Penelope. His beloved wife, just like his country, awaits somewhere beyond the sea, longing for his return just as Odysseus longs to see his dear Ithaca and his family once again. The *Odyssey* is a wonderfully woven story of an unyielding desire to return home despite constant setbacks and hardships. It's also a compelling and engaging narrative full of action and grandiose elements that fascinate readers in the modern world, just as it did in ancient Greece. Despite being a mythical tale, the *Odyssey* is also quite informative, especially in terms of geography around the Mediterranean. In its day, this poem was a valuable source of such information for Greek readers, whereas nowadays, it helps classicists have a better understanding of how much the ancient Greeks knew about the world and how they perceived their region.

Just like the *Iliad,* the final and widely accepted version of the *Odyssey* is divided into 24 books, totaling more than 12,000 lines and covering a comparatively brief part of Odysseus' long journey. Events beyond this short period are also referenced, however, usually through flashbacks. Deities Athena and Poseidon play prominent roles through very dichotomous attitudes and interference in the adventures of Odysseus. Poseidon, begrudged like other gods by the cruel manner in which the Greeks sacked Troy, is a persistent hindrance.

The wrathful sea god also has a personal vendetta against Odysseus due to his fight with Polyphemus, one of the

Cyclopes and a son of Poseidon. He seeks to prevent Odysseus from returning home and torments him and his ship in every way he can during the story. On the contrary, Athena aids the hero through her own interventions, not least of which is her request for Zeus to grant Odysseus his homecoming.

The *Odyssey* begins by describing how the hero's long absence had led the people of his kingdom of Ithaca to assume that he was most likely dead. Apart from the long absence, there was also the fact that all the other great heroes whose fate had predetermined that they would come back home had already found their way, all except Odysseus, who was still being held up by Poseidon. Because of all this, 108 young men had nested themselves in Odysseus' royal palace, spending their riches and all courting Odysseus' wife Penelope, competing for her hand in marriage. Odysseus' clever and courageous son, Telemachus is also introduced early in the poem and given divine instruction from Athena. The instruction was to either find his father or banish the intruders himself and find a worthy new husband for Penelope.

It's impossible to briefly summarize each of the many encounters, detours and stops that Odysseus made during his voyage, but a particularly noteworthy episode was the visit to the Cyclopes. These giants inhabited an island where they lived in peace as sheepherders. Unfortunately, not all of the Cyclopes were so docile, and among them was Poseidon's Polyphemus, a gnarly man-eater who trapped Odysseus and his men in a cave. After Polyphemus started to eat the Greeks, Odysseus devised a plan to get the

Cyclops drunk on wine. As he passed out in his drunken stupor, the Greeks stabbed his single eye and made their escape. This was the slight that made Polyphemus curse Odysseus and pray to Poseidon to make the traveler's voyage a ten-year ordeal.

The subsequent encounters gradually wore down the crew, and Odysseus found himself with an ever-shrinking number of men in his command. The attrition took a major toll by the time Odysseus made his way to Aeaea, the homeland of the witch-like goddess Circe. The dreaded sorceress attacked the party by turning some of Odysseus' men into pigs, but the voyager was able to resolve the dispute when Hermes gifted him a magical plant that provided immunity to Circe's sorcery. Things eventually took a turn, and Odysseus and Circe developed a liking for each other. Whether Penelope would have approved is unknown, but Odysseus and his remaining crew would spend a year on Circe's island, enjoying a much-deserved break from their tumultuous journey. When it came time to move on, Circe advised Odysseus to go down to the underworld and consult with a dead oracle called Tiresias regarding the rest of his path to Ithaca.

As Odysseus descended quite literally to hell, one of the more tragic episodes in the *Odyssey* occurred. The hero runs into his mother Anticlea, learning that she had died from a broken heart after waiting so many years for her son to return from war. It's at this point that Odysseus learns of what had been going on in Ithaca during his long absence. During Odysseus' visit to Hades, Homer also takes an opportunity to revisit many of the legendary heroes who played their parts in the Trojan War and in other Greek myths, such as Achilles and Agamemnon. After having conversations with his war buddies and other legends, Odysseus makes his way back to the realm of the living, getting more valuable advice from Circe for the rest of his voyage.

In all the years that passed, Penelope never gave up hope that Odysseus would return to her, remaining steadfast in her commitment and turning down many offers to remarry. As the hero's long journey approached its conclusion, the situation at the Ithacan royal palace escalated to a point where the suitors plotted to kill Telemachus. Odysseus snuck onto the premises disguised as a beggar, recognized by nobody except the maid Eurycleia, who remembered one of his scars. In a scene worthy of a Hollywood drama movie, Odysseus was also recognized by Argos, his faithful dog that he hero left behind 20 years prior when he set out for war. Unfortunately, the old pooch passed away soon thereafter.

The path Odysseus had to traverse toward eliminating the suitors, reclaiming his rightful throne, and reuniting with Penelope was a journey in itself. The clever Odysseus had to keep a low profile and devise a complex plot, all while enduring abuse from the suitors who perceived him as a raggedy vagrant. The matter was resolved when Penelope hosted an archery challenge, which stipulated that whichever man could string and shoot the old bow of Odysseus would earn the queen's hand. None of the suitors had the necessary strength, and all were shocked when the supposed beggar stepped up and excelled with the bow. It was at this moment that Odysseus revealed his true identity and, as per the plan concocted with his son Telemachus, slaughtered all of the intruders. Toward the end of the story, a minor conflict breaks out between Odysseus and his loyalists and the angered families of the slain suitors. An intervention by Athena and Zeus prevents the war's escalation, and peace is restored over Ithaca under its rightful ruler.

The Argonauts: Jason's Quest for the Golden Fleece

Another major figure among the ancient Greek heroes, perhaps somewhat overshadowed in popular culture by Achilles, Odysseus, and other giants, is Jason. Nonetheless, the legend of Jason and his epic journey with the Argonauts as they searched for the Golden Fleece was and still is among the most popular Greek legends. The story of Jason and the Argonauts is also a pan-Hellenic tale that goes back a long time and predates Homer. Initially passed down as an oral tradition, it was written down and consolidated through various works of ancient Greek literature, such as the *Argonautica* and the Greek tragedy *Medea*.

According to the legends, Jason grew up in the woods around Mount Pelion, where he was tutored by the centaur Cheiron, like Hercules and other greats. His father, Aeson, the king of Iolcus in Thessaly, brought him to the centaur when he was a boy. Traditions also spoke of a glorious and legendary hunt that Jason participated in as a young man alongside other Greek heroes. Some members of the hunting party included Theseus, Atalanta, the Dioscuri brothers (Castor and Polydeuces), and Meleager. Some of these heroes eventually joined the Argonaut expedition with Jason. This hunt from Jason's youth, in pursuit of the mighty Calydonian boar, was one of the earlier adventures his legend was famous for.

Also, in Jason's early life, his father's throne in Iolcus was usurped by the king's half-brother Pelias, who was warned by an oracle that he would one day fall by the blade of a man wearing just one sandal. Wanting to address this injustice, Jason returned home to Iolcus when he turned 20 to reclaim the throne. On the way, Jason lost one of his sandals, which struck fear into Pelias when he saw him enter the city. Wanting to get rid of this foretold threat, Pelias decided to send Jason on a suicide mission, and thus, the quest to find the Golden Fleece began.

The fabled Golden Fleece, which made its way into legend throughout the world, was the prized product of a winged ram that had once belonged to Hermes. The sacred animal came to earth on the instructions of the goddess Nephele, who sent it to evacuate her two children living under the care of their stepmother Ino, the princess of Thebes. The children, Phrixus and Helle were under threat because of Ino's jealousy, as she tried to have them sacrificed. The children then mounted the flying ram and were on their way to safety, but Helle fell off its back during flight, landing in the strait of Dardanelles. When Phrixus landed safely in Colchis on the southeastern coast of the Black Sea, he sacrificed the ram in gratitude to the gods. He then took the animal's Golden Fleece and hung it on an oak tree in one of the sacred groves belonging to the god Ares to be guarded by a serpentine monster.

For the daring task of retrieving this fleece, Athena gave Jason and his entourage a nimble boat built by Argo, a legendary builder. According to the myths, this would be the first long boat commissioned by the Greeks, and it carried the name of its creator. In turn, the heroic expedition was named after the ship. This mighty crew assembled by Jason included some of the most legendary Greek heroes, such as Hercules, but the expedition was still a massive undertaking. After navigating many challenging twists and turns and overcoming a number of enemies, the Argonauts made it to Colchis, at that time ruled by King Aeetes. The king was unwilling to just give the fleece to these foreigners, so the Argonauts had to perform a number of new, difficult tasks. It was during these trials that the enchanting Medea, Aeetes' daughter, came to help the struggling heroes and eventually fell in love with Jason.

Even though the Argonauts fulfilled all of Aeetes' ludicrous requests, which included things like plowing a field with bulls that breathe fire, the king tried to cheat them out of their reward. Fortunately, Medea knew the way to the Golden Fleece and even helped put the fearsome serpent to sleep so that Jason could sneak into the grove and retrieve the treasure. As the Argonauts ran back to their ship, the king sent his troops to stop them, but Medea's magical help once again proved instrumental in fighting them off. Medea boarded the *Argo* with the heroes and left her kingdom to be married to Jason. The way back home to Iolcus was no less adventurous, but the party eventually made it home, where they had to contend with and destroy Pelias since he refused to step down despite being given the Golden Fleece.

In retrospect, there have been two primary areas of discussion regarding the story of Jason and the Golden Fleece. The first concerns the historicity of the tale or, rather, its inspiration from real events. Classicists have suggested that the legend was an amalgamation of real experiences gathered during early naval expeditions carried out by the Greeks out of Mycenae around the 13th century BC. Another major debate has to do with the symbolism of the Golden Fleece, which is widely regarded to be a metaphor. The theories regarding its meaning include royal power, alchemic knowledge, divine forgiveness, wealth, technology, and much more.

Chapter 5: Tragedies and Intrigues

The endless tales that adorn the rich mythology of the ancient Greeks don't end with the gods and the legendary heroes. Quite on the contrary, the gods and the heroes can be seen as something of a nucleus around which countless other epics emerged over the many centuries of cultural development in ancient Greece. Greeks are particularly famous for their dramas, especially ancient Greek tragedies written by the likes of Sophocles, Euripides, and others. Greek tragedians were real trailblazers, and their stories have influenced literature and theater across the world in a profound way. Like all complex societies, the ancient Greeks were also intimately familiar with all things related to political games and palace intrigues among the aristocracy. This, too, is reflected clearly in a lot of their mythology.

Oedipus Rex: The Tragic Fate of Oedipus

Oedipus Rex, sometimes called *Oedipus Tyrannus, Oedipus the King,* or simply *Oedipus,* originally among the ancient Greeks, is one of the most famous Athenian tragedies. Like many other ancient Greek tragedies, *Oedipus Rex* is an adaptation of a pre-existing mythological narrative that the Greek audiences at the time were familiar with. The play is also part of a trilogy about Oedipus that includes *Antigone* and *Oedipus at Colonus,* together sometimes referred to as the three Theban plays of Sophocles.

Antigone was written more than ten years prior to *Oedipus Rex,* but its plot is chronologically the last piece of the trilogy. *Oedipus Rex* was the second to be published, although the events in the play come first in the narrative and are chronologically followed by *Oedipus at Colonus.* *Oedipus Rex* was probably initially known only as *Oedipus* and then renamed to *Oedipus Tyrannus* when *Oedipus at Colonus* came out to make it easier to distinguish between the two. It's also worth noting that the word "tyrant" had a very different meaning in antiquity, simply describing a king who sat on the throne illegitimately and without a proper claim.

The author Sophocles was a highly accomplished man beyond his career as a playwright. He was born into wealth in the community and suburb of Colonus in the wider Athens area. He was a known public figure who held a number of important posts in Athens, particularly his term as the treasurer around 443 BC and, after that, a general. He also had two sons, one with his wife and another with his mistress. Sophocles also made a personal friend of Herodotus, the illustrious historian who is now widely regarded as the "father of history" after being labeled as such by the Romans. Despite his prolific career in politics and aristocratic affairs, these parts of Sophocles' life don't seem to have influenced his writing much.

Oedipus Rex first premiered around 429 BC, and it continues to be performed and adapted into various media to this very day. The play tells the depressing tale of Oedipus, the king of Thebes, and his horrific misfortunes as he unwittingly fulfills a grisly prophecy foretelling that he would kill his father and sleep with his own mother. The story then explores his gradual realization of his terrible predicament and the true nature of his actions, which sends him into a grievous and very dramatic breakdown.

The opening of *Oedipus Rex* paints a grim picture of the city of Thebes, struck by plague and plunged into disorder. The plague wrecks the crops and attacks livestock, while another, more mysterious blight afflicts the city's women in a way that prevents them from having children. A report regarding these hardships is given to King Oedipus by a priest, who also tells him that he must do whatever is necessary to restore normal life. Sophocles then introduces another character, the king's brother-in-law Creon, whom Oedipus had sent to Apollo's temple to consult the god. Creon soon returns to the city and informs the king that the only way to deliver Thebes from its afflictions is to find those responsible for the murder of King Laius, Oedipus's predecessor and, unbeknown to him, his father. The previous king's death is described with a degree of mystery as nobody knows much about the crime except that it was likely the work of robbers.

In an attempt to find answers, Oedipus consults with Tiresias, a blind prophet said to have insights into the knowledge of the god Apollo. When the king and the prophet get to talking, Sophocles elevates the tension by insinuating that the prophet indeed knows the truth of Laius' murder but is, for some reason, afraid to tell Oedipus. The blind man explains that he fears for his safety and that he might die if he speaks. Oedipus is angered by the prophet's reluctance, accusing him of betraying the city for refusing to help lift the pestilence. The king goes as far as to accuse the blind old man of belonging to a plot against Thebes and the crown.

Finally, the prophet yields to the king's insistence and reveals the shocking twist, identifying Oedipus as the killer. Outraged by the accusation of killing the previous king, Oedipus responds with anger and threatens the prophet. Oedipus then also accuses and threatens Creon, but the prophet defends the king's brother-in-law, telling him that Creon had nothing to do with it. With a question, the prophet then implies that Oedipus doesn't truly know who his parents are. He further predicts that Oedipus will soon be struck by the curse of his parents and consequently exiled from the land with "darkness on his eyes."

Still in denial, Oedipus then proceeds to have a conversation with Creon, leveling similar accusations against him and speaking of a plot. The king's wife, Jocasta intervenes on Creon's behalf, refuting Oedipus' claims that her brother was plotting to kill him. Jocasta then begins questioning Oedipus about his visible emotional agony, wanting to know what it was that upset him so much. Oedipus explains that he has been accused of regicide against the late King Laius by Creon and the prophet Tiresias. Comforting him, Jocasta tells Oedipus that the words of prophets shouldn't be taken seriously, recounting how a prophet had once told her and Laius that the king would be slain by his own son. In reality, Jocasta continues, he was killed by brigands "at a place where three roads meet."

Instead of easing Oedipus' racing mind, this story only aggravates his worried curiosity, and he begins inquiring about more details of this place Jocasta spoke of. She describes the fork in the road where Laius was killed in more detail and tells him that one member of the king's party survived the bandit attack. Then, Oedipus tells his wife Jocasta, and the audience, the story of how he came to Thebes and became its king.

Oedipus grew up in Corinth, adopted and raised by King Polybus and his wife, Queen Merope, whom Oedipus assumed were his real parents. As a young man, Oedipus fled Corinth after he began having doubts about his parentage following a strange remark about his father by a random drunkard. Exploring these doubts, he talked to an oracle who told him that he was destined to kill his father and marry his mother, so Oedipus left Corinth to prevent the fulfillment of such a terrible prophecy.

It was during his subsequent travels that Oedipus encountered and, after a dispute, killed an unknown man and much of his entourage. The incident occurred at a fork in the road where a carriage tried to force Oedipus off the road. After killing the driver and the passengers, Oedipus went along his way. When he made it to Thebes, he found that the city was ruled by Creon as a regent due to the death of their king while also contending with the monstrous sphinx attacking the city. After Oedipus helped the defense of Thebes, Creon made him king and encouraged him to marry the former king's widow Jocasta, which Oedipus accepted.

After this bit of background, the story continues with the arrival of a messenger who informs Oedipus about the sudden death of his father in Corinth. For Oedipus, in that moment, the only logical conclusion is that the prophecy he received back in Corinth was false, which was a relief. However, Oedipus still worries about the second half of the prophecy concerning his mother, so the messenger reveals to Oedipus that he needn't worry as he was actually adopted.

The messenger then tells the story of how he was given a baby by a shepherd associated with Laius and told to get rid of it, but he instead brought the baby to Polybus for adoption. Naturally, Oedipus inquires about the shepherd and demands to know who he is, to which he is told that this is the same man who had survived the attack on Laius' carriage. Earlier, when Jocasta mentioned him as a witness, Oedipus had already sent his servants to bring the man for questioning. He had hoped that the man could confirm that Laius was killed by a gang of multiple marauders, which would have cleared Oedipus of the earlier accusations of regicide.

At this point, a terrifying puzzle inches closer to completion. Seeing the writing on the wall, Jocasta pleads with Oedipus to cease his inquiries, believing that his continued ignorance would be a divine blessing compared to the dreadful truth. Oedipus rejects her appeals, and as the shepherd arrives, Jocasta flees the meeting and retires to the royal palace. Like everyone else, the shepherd tries to resist Oedipus' demands to hear the truth, fearing the consequences. After a few threats, the shepherd caves and confirms the messenger's story about the baby that came from Laius.

Sophocles' ensuing description of how the dark truth rips and tears through the lives of all involved and burns Oedipus' entire world to the ground is a masterclass in Greek tragedy. Having learned that he had killed his father and coupled with his own mother, Oedipus demands a sword to put an end to his mother's suffering and presumably to inflict judgment on himself afterward. At this point in the play, a second messenger appears on the stage and brings more tragic news. Paralyzed by grief, Jocasta has hanged herself in her room.

Upon seeing his Jocasta's dangling, lifeless body, Oedipus brings her down and proceeds to gouge his own eyes out. He then decries his cursed fate and that of his poor children, begging to be exiled from the city. Creon enters the stage at this point in the play, trying to figure out what to do. Oedipus requests his own exile, a proper funeral for his mother, and asks Creon to care for his suffering daughters Antigone and Ismene. He expresses hope that they might salvage some semblance of happiness in their lives and somehow rid themselves of their father's misery.

Medea: Revenge of the Sorceress

The tragedy *Medea* premiered in 431 BC, around the same time as *Oedipus Rex,* highlighting this era as a particularly fruitful period for Greek tragedians. *Medea* was written by Euripides, a very prolific dramatist who wrote around 90 plays in total and possibly more than that, with 19 of them being preserved until today. It adapts and tells the epic tale of Medea, the wife of legendary Jason and daughter of King Aeetes of Colchis, the initial keeper of the Golden Fleece. Like the story of Oedipus, the legend of Medea had existed for a long time prior to the writings of Euripides, but the author took certain liberties with the myth and adapted it into a mother's tragedy.

Euripides was lauded by the likes of Aristotle as the most tragic Greek writer of all time, which is an opinion shared by classicists like the famed Edith Hamilton. He never quite received his due praise during his lifetime, but decades and centuries following his death have cemented his legacy across cultures. Euripides lived a much more withdrawn life than Sophocles, coming from a line of priests around Athens.

Medea comes across as a rather simple play at first glance since its entire narrative occurs in Medea's home. The play tells a large story through flashbacks, however, mostly focusing on her life in Colchis prior to meeting Jason and her subsequent move to Corinth in the company of the Argonauts. Different versions of Medea's story describe the events following Medea's immigration to Greece and marriage to Jason differently. Most of the versions involve some form of tragic outcome, particularly the killing of Medea's and Jason's children.

In Euripides' play, things start turning sour when Jason decides that he wants to leave Medea and marry the daughter of King Creon of Corinth, not to be confused with Theban Creon from the story of Oedipus. King Creon was a powerful man ruling a powerful polity, so marrying the princess would have been a powerful leap for Jason. As such, the story presents him as a callous rogue who moves to abandon his loving wife and their two sons for selfish reasons. Perhaps owed to Jason's legendary status after having recovered the Golden Fleece, Creon was quite happy to marry his daughter to the hero.

Euripides' *Medea* begins with a description of a broken and visibly unstable woman, crying in her home due to her husband's callousness. This opening scene takes place shortly after Medea was first informed that Jason was planning to leave her and remarry into the king's family. The nurse employed to help with the unfortunate couple's two sons addresses the audience and laments Medea's sorry state. The nurse takes note of the hatred that seems to be growing in Medea's heart, and she expresses concern that her mistress might do something drastic. She worries especially about the children since it appears that Medea now hates them. The nurse exchanges these concerns with the children's tutor, who feels the same way, and they decide to try and keep the children away from Medea while she is beside herself with grief.

The next scene shows Medea cursing her family and house, referring to her sons as the "accursed children of a hated mother." She even wishes them to be "done for along with their father." Medea also wishes death upon herself, lamenting before the gods Themis and Artemis and asking them to destroy her home. Euripides takes this opportunity to comment on gender relations and roles, having Medea address all the women of Corinth in a speech about men. Casting doubt on the notion that women enjoy themselves in the security of their homes while men go off to war, Medea says that she would rather go into battle than give birth. Furthermore, she compares herself to "pirate loot" in the way she was brought by Jason from a foreign land.

After this dramatic rant, King Creon enters the stage and tells Medea that she is to be exiled from Corinth. He plainly tells her that he fears she might kill his daughter or exact some other retribution on her. Medea tries to reason with the king, assuring him that Jason is the sole object of her scorn, not his would-be bride. Unrelenting, Creon repeats his order and tells Medea that he will use force if necessary. Unable to change the king's mind, Medea feigns capitulation and asks for just one more day so that she can prepare for the journey and secure her children. Fatefully, the king accepts this request. As Creon departs the scene, Medea declares her intention to kill him, his daughter, and Jason.

The following scene features Jason, who comes up to Medea to assure her that even though he's leaving and exiling her, she will be provided for. He says he won't allow her to end up poor, which could be interpreted as a bribe to make her go away. This probably only adds insult to injury, and Medea calls him a cheater and a rat, an ungrateful one at that, since she was instrumental in helping Jason acquire the Golden Fleece before leaving her homeland for him. Jason then tells her that he has come to despise her and that this was her fault, but he reiterates he will do right by her in divorce. He urges her to let go of her anger and accept his offer, otherwise she is a fool.

Soon thereafter, King Aegeus of Athens, sympathetic to Medea's plight, offers her asylum in Athens. With a route of escape now set, Medea addresses the audience yet again, explaining her plan to begin poisoning her enemies. Feigning forgiveness, she tells Jason that she wishes him luck and presents a fine dress for his future wife as her gift and symbol of goodwill. Jason is glad to see that Medea is starting to see reason, completely unaware that the dress was a delivery device for a vicious poison. After that, Medea decides and announces that she will kill her sons as well, lamenting with grief that she must do this terrible deed.

Medea then informs her husband and children that she is no longer wrathful, asking for the children to stay with Jason, after which her gifts are sent to the princess of Corinth. Medea rationalizes her decision to kill her two boys as a way of preventing their abuse and torment at the hands of her enemies after she is exiled. Soon enough, a messenger arrives and informs Medea that Creon and his daughter are dead, to which Medea rejoices. All that's left after that is to put down the children and leave Corinth, and the grisly murder occurs behind the stage.

Jason soon arrives, holding the sword that had seemingly slain his children. Their murderous mother starts hovering over her unfaithful husband, accompanied by the bodies of their sons. One last time, Jason laments Medea's dreadful nature, calling her a thing of hate and a woman most loathsome to the gods, to himself, and to all of humanity. Medea tells him that all this death was his own doing, even refusing to give him the bodies of the boys to bury, choosing instead to bury them herself at Hera's shrine. The vicious vengeance is completed by allowing Jason to go on living without a wife and without his children, and the enchantress of Colchis flies away.

House of Atreus: Agamemnon, Clytemnestra, and the Curse

While not a specific piece of written drama, the dark story of Mycenaean King Atreus and his cursed family is an essential tale of Greek mythology that has inspired quite a few works of literature in its time. The story was also familiar to the Romans, who adopted it into their own literature. Given the gravity of the legend, it usually inspired tragedies. Some of the most famous examples include the trilogy of *Oresteia* by the Greek tragedian Aeschylus and *Thyestes* by the Roman philosopher and dramatist Seneca. Aeschylus and Seneca wrote their plays around five centuries apart, respectively in the 5th century BC and the 1st century AD, illustrating just how enduring and timeless the stories of Atreus were.

The consequences of the hereditary curse are no less dreadful than its causes, and the entire ordeal lasted five generations. It was an era of bloodletting involving murder and revenge passed down like an inherited disease in the bloodline. The curse began with Atreus' grandfather and founder of the House of Atreus, King Tantalus. Tantalus committed a terrible sacrilege against the gods by taking it upon himself to test their omniscience. Doubting the gods and giving into fateful curiosity was bad enough, but Tantalus took things to the extreme by deciding that the best way to test divine omniscience was to serve pieces of his son Pelops to them for dinner.

The king's misguided idea was to chop Pelops up into little pieces and try to trick the gods into eating the flesh unknowingly, thus proving that they didn't know everything. When Tantalus offered his feast to the gods, they expectedly realized that it was made up of the boiled pieces of Pelops. Rightfully outraged, the gods would enact a trans-generational retribution on Tantalus and his progeny in the form of a curse.

King Atreus' part in the curse was to get embroiled in a prolonged rivalry with his brother Thyestes that ended in blood. The vicious cycle of revenge even saw Atreus killing and cooking Thyestes' son before tricking him into eating their flesh. Atreus was eventually murdered by Aegisthus, another secret son of Thyestes, by his own daughter Pelopia. The next to suffer the consequences was King Agamemnon, the famous leader of the Greek war against Troy and a son to Atreus along with Menelaus. Agamemnon's fate was to be killed by his wife Clytemnestra, the sister of the legendary beauty Helen, who married Menelaus and was later taken by Paris of Troy.

Agamemnon's undoing started while he was off fighting the Trojan War, during which time Clytemnestra began cheating on him with Aegisthus. Agamemnon's wife didn't start an affair out of boredom, though. Following Agamemnon's sacrifice of their daughter Iphigenia to Artemis just to enable his fleet to cross the sea, Clytemnestra had every reason to be bitter toward her husband. On top of that, Agamemnon himself also cheated, returning from the war with Cassandra at his side. Seeing this, Clytemnestra finally decided to kill Agamemnon. She then proceeded to clean house by killing Cassandra and having Aegisthus slaughter Agamemnon's guards, after which the queen and her lover took over the kingdom. These events forced Agamemnon's only son, Orestes into exile.

Orestes only survived, thanks to his sister Electra, who helped smuggle him out of the palace following the coup. Growing up in a foreign land, Orestes plotted vengeance like many of the Atreidai before him. However, Orestes wasn't happy or eager to carry out this revenge since it would involve the killing of his own mother. Unsure of the right course, Orestes consulted an oracle of Apollo for advice. The god confirmed that avenging his father was his duty, failing, which would result in grave consequences for Orestes.

Apollo's answer was clear, and Orestes eventually mustered up the strength to go back to Mycenae and kill his mother and Aegisthus. The mission was a success, but unlike many of his malicious ancestors and relatives, Orestes was emotionally tormented by his crime. Clytemnestra had indeed committed a terrible act in killing her husband, but so had Orestes. Following the killings, Orestes wandered the earth, wallowing in his guilt and dangling on the edge of insanity. Apollo eventually took pity on the mortal, helping set up a divine trial for Orestes in Athens where he could be either punished or absolved to receive closure. Presiding over the process was the goddess Athena, and the council eventually found Orestes not guilty of anything.

More importantly, this ruling finally lifted the curse that had tormented House Atreus for five generations.

Chapter 6: The Underworld and Beyond

Like all developed cultures in human history, the ancient Greeks were captivated by the questions posed by death, particularly notions about the afterlife. Greek mythology is well known for having quite a few things to say about the underworld, as embodied by Hades. Both a god and a place, Hades featured many other mythological aspects within it, describing much of the process of dying and passing on to the other side. Styx, herself also a goddess and a place (river) at the same time, played a pivotal role in that system.

As one of the most famous mythical places in the Greek tradition, Hades was featured in many stories and was the location of various events described in Greek mythology. Numerous mortals and demigods would occasionally wander into the dark halls of Hades before coming back to the living realm. Apart from the adventures of Odysseus that led him to the depths of hell, another famous story of an incursion into Hades was that of Orpheus, the Argonaut hero who descended to the realm below for love.

Hades, God of the Underworld

Quite a few of the stories covered thus far overlap with some aspects of Hades. This god was particularly important for the ancient Greeks, which is why he's an ever-present factor in the fates of so many other gods and legendary figures in Greek mythology. Across different Greek myths that might be as dissimilar as possible, Hades is often the figure that hovers over the events or rather lurks below them. The importance of Hades was enough to make the Romans adopt the same concept, often referencing the god of the underworld in many of their own myths, traditions, and religious practices. To the Romans, Hades was known as Pluto. Still, Hades doesn't feature as a protagonist in mythological tales as often as the other Olympians, but his mere association with the final destination that souls go to was enough to make him essential.

At the same time, Hades was the name and embodiment of the great dark expanse that lay beneath the known world, far removed from the worldly affairs of mortals and even from the Olympian gods. Yet despite his remoteness, Hades was always present in spirit and in the minds of people. This is because Hades was the final stop for every soul after the passing of their mortal body, an unavoidable end that every man, woman, and child would eventually meet.

Due to his strong association with the world of the dead, Hades was often given many negative connotations in the world of the mortals. This is especially apparent in the writings of Hesiod and Homer, who variously described the god of the underworld as having no pity and being a monster. Many ancient Greeks uttered the name of Hades with reluctance and unease, often preferring to use some of his various epithets instead. Talking too much about Hades was often seen as inviting bad luck and simply asking for trouble, making Hades the object of much superstition. Among the gods, perhaps the most controversial aspect of

Hades was his relationship with Persephone, his abducted wife and daughter of the agricultural goddess Demeter.

Hades came to rule the underworld in the aftermath of the Olympian war against the Titans. After the victory, Zeus and his brothers Poseidon and Hades divided up the world among themselves through a random selection process. They drew lots to see who'd get to rule which part, and Hades was thus assigned the underworld. One of the more famous legends about Hades was that of his invisibility cap or helmet, designed and built by Hephaestus. This single item is featured in a number of stories as an instrumental tool in helping other gods or legendary heroes reach their goals. The previously discussed story of Perseus is one example, but the cap is also mentioned in the *Iliad,* where Athena used it in her conflict with Ares.

The god Hades was widely featured in various forms of ancient Greek art, especially mosaics, pottery illustrations, and sculptures. He is usually portrayed as a mature, masculine figure, in contrast to the likes of Apollo, who was always represented as a strikingly beautiful and very young man. Hades tend to feature a full beard, typically holding a scepter, bident, a two-pronged spear, or something similar. It's also common to see Hades accompanied by Cerberus, sitting at the god's side as his fearsome but loyal pooch. In other portrayals, Hades sits on a throne made of ebony or drives a chariot with a string of black horses. Important events associated with Hades have also been portrayed, such as his abduction of Persephone or their marriage.

Hades was one of the unfortunate sons of Cronus, spending a portion of his early life in his father's stomach. As the first-born son of Cronus and Rhea, he spent the longest time in this dreadful trap among all his siblings. Hades also had three sisters, including Hestia, Hera, and Demeter. After Zeus made Cronus regurgitate the sons he had devoured, the active role of Hades among the Greek deities began alongside his brother Poseidon.

In Hades' realm beneath the earth, two other deities played pivotal roles in the travel of souls into this dark world. Traditions state that Hermes, the messenger, guided the souls along the early part of the trip, which ended at the river Styx. Crossing this river was the essential step these souls had to take to find their resting place in Hades. Their passage was the responsibility of ferryman Charon, who commanded the infamous Dead Souls Express. After traversing the river, Charon would direct the souls to the gates of Hades, where Cerberus would stare them down before finally entering the underworld.

To modern sensibilities, Hades as a place certainly resembles hell, but that's not necessarily what the ancient Greeks intended. It's likely that the underworld and its associated god were seen negatively simply because of their connection to death. While most cultures and religions offer some way for human beings to cope with their mortality and eventual death by embellishing it, it's safe to say that death tends to be seen negatively overall. The ancient Greeks were no different, so the dread and anxiety with which they looked upon Hades might have had more to do with their disdain for death than a desire to punish sinful souls in the afterlife. That's not to say that some of the figures in Greek mythology didn't suffer in Hades, but the nature of this place is largely ambiguous in terms of how it felt to those resting there. Rather than constructing an eternal dungeon of torment for those who transgressed in this life, the Greeks merely sought to give all passing souls a place of final rest.

More troubling for the Greeks was the idea of an improper burial, and this is reflected in their stories of Hades. The common ritual was for those burying a family member or friend to leave a coin for Charon, usually placed in the deceased's mouth, as a payment for ferrying their souls across the Styx. Failing this could result in the soul of the departed wandering across the world in the form of ghosts. The same fate would befall the unburied, which made funeral processions extremely important to all pious Greeks. This is one of the reasons why the *Iliad* makes such an enormous motif of Achilles' abuse of Hector's corpse. The Romans later expanded on this aspect of the myth in interesting ways. According to Vergil's *Aeneid,* those who were homeless or friendless or simply had no money wouldn't always wander. Sometimes, they'd make it to the Styx but would have to wait a hundred years at its shore.

The River Styx, Cerberus, and the Judgment of Souls

Even though all the souls went to the same place, Greek mythology definitely provided concepts regarding the judgment of souls in the afterlife. This judgment began at the gates, where a mortal soul was analyzed regarding the individual's actions during their time on earth. The result of this assessment decided the exact final destination the soul would go to within Hades. Like many stories in Greek mythology, the process varies somewhat across sources, but the most widely accepted tradition spoke of three judges, including Rhadamanthus, Aeacus, and Minos. The judges would hold court in the proximity of the Palace of Hades and Persephone. All three judges were once mortal themselves, ruling as kings in their respective Greek polities. It is said that they became judges in Hades by virtue of their righteous lives.

After the judgment, souls were divided into two groups based on whether they did good or evil in their lives. The most righteous of the souls were first brought to the river Lethe, which was also described as a pool of water in some interpretations. Drinking from this divine water allowed the virtuous departed to wipe their minds clean of all the memories of evil and pain. Once cleansed to perfection, they would move on to the Elysian Fields. The idyllic Elysium was variously described as a plain, field, or group of islands known as the Islands of the Blessed, where the virtuous could begin anew.

On the other hand, the evildoers were placed in the custody of Furies and taken to the depths of Tartarus, perhaps to endure certain punishments. The Greeks also envisioned eternal torment for particularly evil souls, especially those who offended the gods. These eternal punishments correspond to what might be defined today as "personal hell," with tailored retribution inflicted on each of the condemned based on their misdeeds. One very famous example of such a punishment was the endless suffering of Sisyphus, who was condemned to push a boulder uphill only to have it slide back down to be pushed again in perpetuity. A third category of judgment was also envisioned for those who had traveled a moral middle path in life. These souls would be returned to the Fields or Meadows of Asphodel, the first and closest region of Hades.

Clearly, the Greek underworld was home to all sorts of creatures and deities other than Hades, often playing their own roles in the process of a mortal's passing. One such god is Styx, who, similarly to Hades, represents both a deity and a place or, more precisely a river. Although she was a Titan, Styx was held in high regard among the Olympian gods due to her assistance in the Titanomachy. After Styx, Cerberus is perhaps the most famous of the underworld creatures. Dead souls on their way to Hades would eventually pass this vigilant guardian on their way, but Cerberus was there to ensure they could never leave. The three-headed dog's secondary role was to keep living mortals from entering, although some of the stories described exceptions to this rule.

Styx was born to the mighty Titan Oceanus, one of the ancient ones. Her mother was Tethys, sister and wife to Oceanus. Styx was also one of the Oceanids, the three thousand nymph daughters of Oceanus and Tethys. According to Hesiod, Styx married Pallas, another Titan with whom she had four children, including Zelus (Glory or Rivalry), Nike (Victory), Kratos (Strength or Dominion), and Bia (Force). Apart from her role in the procession of dead souls and her part in stories like the near-immortalization of Achilles who was dipped in her waters, the mythology of Styx had other important elements.

The interpretation of Styx as both a goddess and a river is owed to the epithets given to her by various Greek writers. These epithets also show that she was often associated with terms like hatred and abhorrence. Styx was variously described as terrible and formidable, not necessarily to express disdain but simply to highlight her awesome presence and power. The waters of Styx were said to be cold and "down-flowing." That Greeks weren't repulsed by Styx is illustrated by Hesiod's detailed descriptions of the goddess in her personified form. He wrote that she lived a life separate from that of the other gods, occupying a "glorious house upon great rocks and propped up to heaven." He also described her domicile as adorned by silver pillars. It's clear from the writings that Styx was still seen as an elegant, divine, and beautiful incarnation like most goddesses.

As for the body of water, the Greeks believed that Styx, like other rivers, flowed from the great and primordial Ocean River that enveloped the world and gave life to all the smaller ones. This origin is embodied in the fact that Oceanus was Styx's father. The description of Styx as water acquired new details and even different interpretations over time, with some later Greek writers like Plato describing it as a lake. The story of Achilles being dipped into Styx also signifies that Greeks sometimes saw the waters of Styx as an elixir of immortality, which is a frequent element in mythologies around the world.

Last but not least, one of the most important roles of the Styx was as a place of oaths for the other gods. Essentially, whenever a god needed to make some kind of Oath, they would either invoke the name of Styx or physically acquire her water to perform an oath ritual, depending on the version. In some retellings, a god looking to make an oath would send a messenger such as Iris to go down to Styx and take some of her water into a golden jug. The liquid would then be used as a libation for the god to pour out of the jug while making their oath. Making an oath in the name of Styx was a big deal among the Olympians, showing that even the gods had to observe certain rules.

Upholding these oaths was a sacred duty, and whichever god dared break such an oath would be punished. The punishment involved two stages, the first consisting of one full year of sickness. In a state of broken spirit, unable to breathe, and prohibited from tasting ambrosia or nectar, a punished god would lie in a strewn bed, all while enduring a powerful trance. After a year has passed in this sorry state, the god would be ostracized for a full nine years, unable to participate in any activities with the other gods of Olympus. Only in the tenth year would they be welcomed back into regular divine affairs and once more invited to feasts, councils, and other meetings.

Regarding the dreaded Cerberus, he received a few different descriptions over time. The most enduring portrayal is that of the three-headed guard dog monster, but some chroniclers like Hesiod described him as having 50 heads and serpents protruding from his body. The most famous myth involving the Hound of Hades, as Cerberus is often called, is the earlier-discussed twelfth labor of Hercules. Each of the three heads of Cerberus featured terrifying fangs, enough to devour anybody trying to escape or enter Hades without permission. Some of the myths also spoke of the hound's ability to secrete venom. This comes from the story of how Medea tried to poison Theseus in Athens. The poison was extracted from the saliva of Cerberus, which, according to legend, spilled all over the world as Hercules dragged the ferocious beast on a leash after his triumph.

Orpheus and Eurydice, a Love That Defies Death

Not all major figures of Greek mythology, whether deities or legendary heroes, were meant to embody combat skills or power. They shared a lot of the same attributes, but not all of them became famous just for fighting monsters and pursuing glory. There were also myths that tended to focus on some of the nicer things in life, involving heroes motivated by things like love and beauty. The ancient Greeks clearly held storytelling and the arts in very high regard, which is why some of their mythical characters were created and developed to represent the height of such endeavors. Orpheus is perhaps the most famous example of this, known as the most perfect musician, singer, poet, orator, and prophet to have ever lived.

This legendary virtuoso was said to have no match when it came to playing the lyre, which became his symbol. Orpheus' melodies were so enchanting that they spoke to wildlife, charmed the plants and trees, and could even make streams stop to listen to his voice and music. Although a deeply artistic soul, Orpheus was certainly no less heroic than the other major figures of Greek mythology. He played a part in the epic Argonaut adventure right alongside Jason in his search for the Golden Fleece. Most famously, however, Orpheus dove into the depths of Hades to find and rescue his beloved wife, Eurydice.

Orpheus came from a line of similarly talented figures, including his father, Apollo, the undisputed finest musician in the universe. His mother was Calliope, the Muse of epic poetry. There are also versions that cite Orpheus' father as the mortal King Oeagrus of Thrace. Coincidentally, Thrace is also the place where the ancient Greeks thought the lyre originated. Orpheus also had a brother by the name of Linus, the ill-fated but celebrated musician and orator who met a tragic end at the hands of Hercules, whom he had been tutoring in music.

After spending a period of his life in Egypt, Orpheus joined the Argonauts upon his return to Greece. Among the members of the legendary expedition, Orpheus would often take it upon himself to lift the spirits of the *Argo's* crew. He provided entertainment on their long journey and kept their mood up even when the going got tough. Orpheus' beloved music even helped mend conflicts among the Argonauts, preventing fights and maintaining the party's cohesion. Since his music was so beautiful that it affected the natural world, Orpheus could even secure calmer seas with his singing voice and placate monsters such as the Sirens. There's hardly another story that better communicates just how much the ancient Greeks loved and respected the art of music.

In a way, the life of Orpheus revolved around a woman, as his love for Eurydice was the stuff of legend. Infrequently called Agriope as well, Eurydice was one of the Auloniads, the nymphs of mountain pastures and heavily associated with nature. Unfortunately, this was to be a tragic love hindered by challenges. According to widely accepted traditions, Eurydice was attacked by Aristaeus not long after she married Orpheus. Aristaeus had become infatuated with the nymph and, in his attempt to pursue her, began chasing her. During the chase, Eurydice stepped on a viper, which bit her ankle and promptly killed her. There are different versions regarding when exactly this happened, with some sources claiming it was on the couple's wedding night.

Orpheus was naturally devastated, but he refused to let that be the end of their love. He quickly followed his wife down to Hades, armed not with a sword or a club but with his music. When he reached the Styx, Orpheus played such a beautiful song that Charon, the dreaded boatman, ferried him across the river for free. The hero next faced the three snarling heads of the fearsome Cerberus, who would not let a living soul enter the realm of death. Fortunately, even a feared monstrosity such as Cerberus was no match for Orpheus' notes and voice, and the beast soon yielded to his charms.

The first authority figure Orpheus met was Hades' wife Persephone, whom he pleaded with to release his wife back to life. Hades himself soon emerged, and even his cold, dead heart was touched by Orpheus' predicament. As the gods were reluctant to make such an enormous exception and let a mortal come back to life, Orpheus offered to simply stay in Hades so he could live next to his beloved wife. His commitment and love for Eurydice were enough to convince the gods to let Eurydice go.

Unfortunately, the story would reach a tragic conclusion. The gods agreed to let them both go, but releasing a deceased soul from Hades was no simple matter. The gods told Orpheus that he should head back to the living realm and trust them that Eurydice's shadow would follow right behind him so that they could be reunited on the surface. The only catch was that he wasn't allowed to glance back at her until they both fully left Hades. Otherwise, she would stay in Hades forever. Orpheus then headed back, but since Eurydice was still in her shadow form, she made no sound. Unable to resist the suspicion that the gods had cheated him and that Eurydice wasn't behind him, Orpheus looked back. He caught but a glance of his wife's shadowy eyes before she vanished forever just as they were both about to exit the shadow realm.

As he reentered the living world again, Orpheus still found himself alone. An unrelenting, debilitating grief took hold of him, and, in his hopelessness, Orpheus was unable to eat or drink for quite a while. After regaining some semblance of stability, he began to walk the earth, wandering through Thrace in an aimless drift. Legends say that he no longer wanted anyone's company and would never sing or play music again. Soon thereafter, Orpheus met his end at the hands of the Thracian Maenads, the fanatical female worshipers of Dionysus who tore the tragic hero into pieces.

Chapter 7: Influence on Culture

To say that Greek mythology has influenced the shared culture of humanity would be a severe understatement. This is especially apparent in the Western world in the broadest sense. The ancient Romans, who found themselves in the immediate vicinity of Greece and eventually absorbed its territories, were fascinated with all things Hellenic. As proud and powerful as the Romans were, they never made any secret of this. In fact, they were happy to adopt major portions of Greek mythology, culture, art styles, philosophy, architecture, and much more, taking these influences and molding them into their own, different society.

In turn, subsequent Western cultures have absorbed a lot of influence from both of these Mediterranean civilizations, leading to a sort of fusion between Greek and Roman mythology over time. This confluence gave rise to the study of classicism as one whole, which is why the term classical mythology is often used to refer to the combined mythologies of Rome and Greece. One should also always note that cultural influence, exchange, and heritage happen in an endless continuity, and even the most influential cultural centers, like ancient Greece, had been somewhat shaped by others. In the case of Greece, such exchanges occurred mostly with ancient Mesopotamia, North Africa (Egypt), and other locales where early civilizations sprouted. This cultural continuity has never relented to this very day, and tidbits of ancient Greek myths and concepts can be found in anything from literature to advertising and even the most basic popular culture.

Greek Mythology in Literature, Art, and Philosophy

From the very beginning, Greek mythology has occupied a prominent place in literature, art, and philosophy. The most obvious place where this happened was ancient Greece, as their mythology was an omnipresent thread that weaved its way through almost everything that the Greeks did. The body of Greek literature featuring motifs from mythology extends far beyond the works cited and discussed in this book, but the poems and plays described are among the most famous and influential.

Mythology was a common topic of discussion and exploration among the ancient Greeks, influencing a lot of their famous philosophy. Because of this and religion, mythology was also present in politics as a source of inspiration, role models, ideals, and much more. The relationship between famous Greek philosophers like Socrates, Plato, and Aristotle is a complex issue. Socrates is particularly problematic because of the so-called Socratic problem, which is a historiographical term referring to the difficulty that historians have had in establishing a clear set of the beliefs and thoughts of Socrates. This is because Socrates kept no written documentation of anything he taught. What is known about his philosophy comes from his pupils, some of whom include equally famous philosophers like Plato. Plato learned directly from Socrates as his pupil, and some of the teachings were then passed down from Plato to other greats like Aristotle, who learned from Plato.

Quite famously, Socrates was tried and sentenced to death for allegedly corrupting the youth in Athens. It's unclear whether he challenged the very existence of the gods or practiced religion while simply being a critic, but his judges accused him of impiety. Further complicating things is the fact that religion was rather fragmented in ancient Greece, subject to all sorts of variations and local or even personal practices, as mentioned earlier. Generally, there wasn't a well-established, firm dogma upheld by a church-like institution. What is known is that Greek polytheism and its associated myths played a major role in Socrates' philosophy. One recorded thought of his was that goodness or virtue was independent of the deities and his insistence that gods, too, have to be pious and observe their own rules.

Plato also dabbled in mythology in his philosophy, believing strongly in the virtue of the gods. He thought them to be good and separated their influence from all evil in man, stating that the goodness in mankind was the work and responsibility of the gods while evil wasn't. On the other hand, Aristotle was famously and quite extremely critical of Greek religion. His critique of the myths was an important aspect of his work, as Aristotle believed the traditional myths to be absurd and rejected the very existence of gods.

After a long period in which classical antiquity didn't enjoy much of the limelight in the European mainstream, a massive cultural shift would burst onto the stage in the 15th

century. Nowadays referred to as the Renaissance, the period that began around the late 15th century brought a massive resurgence of interest in classicism. This outbreak of fascination with antiquity and its myths was particularly pronounced in paintings and other visual arts. Pivotal moments in Greek mythology were frequently depicted, some of them numerous times by different artists, a practice that would continue well after the Renaissance.

One especially popular motif that cropped up time and time again among painters was the story of Cronus devouring his sons. Francisco Goya's *Saturn Devouring His Son* and Peter Paul Rubens' *Saturn* are especially shocking and unnerving portrayals. Named as such after the Roman version of Cronus, both of these adaptations are equally terrifying in their own unique ways, mostly owed to the all-too-human interpretation of the myth. In the traditional narrative, the story is certainly unsettling but unrealistic enough for comfort. After all, the original Cronus or Saturn simply gulps his children down, swallows them whole, and eventually spits them out alive.

In the paintings, however, the dreadful god bites, tears, and chews his victims. Rubens' interpretation from 1636 is mainly unsettling because of its realism. It depicts Cronus as an old, grey man biting and tearing at the skin of one of his babies as the child cries in agony, in a rather terrifying bit of artistic liberty in relation to the original myth. Goya's depiction, which was painted in the early 1820s, is just as horrific. It features less realism regarding the anatomy of Saturn, but the derangement infused into the character by Goya is truly an unsettling sight. Although it doesn't depict a baby, the painting is even gorier than that of Rubens because it features an anatomically correct body of a grown man being torn limb from limb and with its head missing while blood pours down from the mangled flesh.

What might have possessed artists to put a much darker spin on such stories is anybody's guess, but the evolution of these portrayals is fascinating to study. Of course, Cronus is just one of many motifs that have inspired an endless range of artworks over the centuries. The entrance of Theseus into the labyrinth while receiving help from Ariadne is another moment from mythology that has been immortalized in quite a few artistic renditions.

Modern Adaptations and Interpretations

In today's world, adaptations and interpretations of Greek motifs have made it into virtually every medium of art and entertainment and well beyond. Music, films, novels, video games, and many other creative outlets are consistently receiving new material inspired by ancient Greece. The advent of film has been particularly interesting for Greek mythology enthusiasts since its inception because it provided a whole new way of retelling the stories and presenting them in a novel, visual manner.

In the early 21st century, such projects took on an extreme scale, famously exemplified by the 2004 epic *Troy*. Although it received a lot of criticism for the liberties the script took with Homer's *Iliad*, the project was a massive commercial success. With an all-star lineup of Hollywood actors and intense visuals, the movie's production ended up costing around $185 million. Even though it was one of the most expensive movies in history then, the box office profits would almost quadruple the investment. Brad Pitt and company probably had a lot to do with that, but the movie's success was an unquestionable testament to the popularity of the subject matter as well.

Present-day interpretations of Greek mythology can sometimes run rather wild, which has resulted from a prolonged process of analysis and new understanding. In modern times, scholars and thinkers have made a lot of effort since the late 18th century to properly interpret Greek mythology following its revival. The end of the 18th century was roughly the time when interest in Greek mythology began to spread to the wider masses in Europe.

The early days mostly focused on understanding the myths and their purpose, but with time, people began to put their own spin on the stories. An interesting genre worth exploring is the retelling of Greek myths. These often come in the form of novels that tell the old stories from a new perspective, such as that of a new character. Technology has made the creative process easier than ever, so the Internet is full of all sorts of interpretations and spinoffs. If one would be so inclined, it might be possible to read the retelling of the *Iliad* from a lowly soldier's perspective or another creative exploration of other myths along those lines. Similarly, retellings and adaptations in theaters all across the world are some of the best ways to experience, preserve, and expand upon Greek mythology. After all, the Greeks pioneered this art form, and their influence has been further magnified through early modern-era greats like Shakespeare, who drew heavy influence from Greek tragedies.

Greek Mythology in Popular Culture

Ever since the Renaissance restored classical antiquity to glory, there has been an endless torrent of Greek elements cropping up in every corner of the Western cultural experience. Greek myths, aesthetics, legends, and philosophies are so influential that it's difficult to go outside in any European city without running into at least a minor trace of ancient Greek heritage. These are usually small things that most people either don't know or simply don't notice because they are routine.

Even a regular doctor visit in today's world is likely to expose an individual to Greek mythology. The famous international symbol of medical science, the serpent slithering around a staff, was originally a Greek symbol representing Asclepius, the god of medicine. Ancient Greek statues created in honor of this god feature the typical anthropomorphic incarnation of a deity, showing a man holding a staff with a snake entwined around it. Just like today, medical doctors in ancient Greece were held in very high regard across society, although Greek doctors were usually priests of Asclepius who engaged in various forms of healing.

Psychology in the West also abounds in motifs from Greek mythology, with famous examples like the so-called Oedipus complex as presented by Sigmund Freud. Similar concepts include the Medea complex and the Electra complex. Similar influences can be found in biology, where elements of Greek mythology are featured in many technical terms, concepts, theories, and other instances.

References to Greek mythology are especially prevalent in astronomy and astrology. Constellations, planets, and other celestial bodies were often named in reference to ancient Greece, including examples like Capricorn, Scorpius, the 1108 Demeter asteroid, and many others. Among all things related to space, perhaps the most famous tribute to Greek mythology was the Apollo program, which took multiple human beings to the moon. The name wasn't chosen at random, referring to Apollo's legendary archery skills and incredible accuracy, as well as his association with knowledge and light.

In general, symbols used in virtually all areas of life in the West are brimming with Greek mythological connections. Company logos and advertising, for instance, often use such motifs, which further illustrates how ubiquitous and recognizable many elements of Greek mythology are. It's no accident that Nike, perhaps the biggest brand in sports apparel, was named after the goddess of victory. The list of such examples can go on for days. Whether it's in business brands, science, art, geography, entertainment, advertising, or even Internet memes, Greek mythology is bound to show up sooner or later if one cares to look.

It's also worth noting that these mythological elements weren't always so prevalent or even welcomed. Nowadays, they find their way into popular culture without much of a reaction or interest, but during the Middle Ages in Europe, references to pre-Christian, pagan traditions were strongly discouraged and suppressed. This was apparent in the era's literature and art, but the Renaissance changed everything. During this time, the fascination with all things related to classical antiquity took the continent by storm and became a true cultural phenomenon. It's difficult to predict what would have happened to with all this Greek influence without the Renaissance, but it's safe to say that it helped normalize such heritage. As a result, Greek mythology is now widely accepted as an integral part of common European heritage.

Impact on Western Cultural Imagination

Across the Western world, Greek mythology has been around for so long and influenced so much that it has entrenched itself deep into the collective subconscious of societies across many centuries. What this means is that Greek mythology and its associated narratives have affected many facets of the collective Western mentality if such a thing can be said to exist. Cultural imagination itself is difficult to define, but it could be seen as the combined sum of views, discussions, philosophy, intellectual pursuits, and cultural zeitgeists.

One thing to consider is the extensive linguistic influence of ancient Greece. For instance, the very word "history" is rooted in the ancient Greek word *historía,* which denotes an inquiry or knowledge accrued through investigation. Examples of such words are endless, including mathematics, philosophy, music, and about 3.6% of the 500 most common English words today. English is certainly not an isolated case in this regard, as things like history, mathematics, music, and philosophy are often called similarly in many Indo-European languages with some audible variation in pronunciation.

This linguistic residue left behind by the ancient Greeks is taken for granted and routinely overlooked, but its implications are immense. The word "music" has traveled a long way across cultures and centuries to make it to its current English form, passing through a line of precursors in Old English, Old French, and Latin, all of which descend from the ancient Greek word *mousiké*. The clue as to the relevance of mythology becomes quite apparent upon closer inspection, and it's easy to tell that the word references the Muses even if the observer doesn't speak a word of Greek. Specifically, the word means "art of the Muses," referring to the nine goddesses of inspiration that presided over the arts and sciences. What this means is that people all over the world constantly speak tidbits of ancient Greek in their daily lives without even realizing it, and therein lies the secret of the eternal cultural endurance of ancient Greece. Latin has had similar powers for a very long time, especially in science.

Language is an incredibly powerful influence in shaping cultures and societies, along with their mentalities, conventions, relationships, spirituality, and much more. The entrenching of Greek mythology goes beyond mere words, though, as the words themselves are sometimes tied to concepts or entire stories behind them. Take the adjective "herculean" as an example. On the surface, it's a term that simply alludes to Hercules' strength, but it carries with it a whole string of stories and adventures associated with the hero. The more familiar one becomes with the background, the more weight such words attain.

Beyond linguistics and their consequences, the stories and characters of Greek mythology have influenced aspects of morality, storytelling, and a whole range of concepts in human behavior and values, such as heroism, sacrifice, love, greed, patriotism, nostalgia, and much more. If there is a feature of the human experience and emotional or moral depth to be listed, then there's probably also a Greek myth that connects to it. The Greeks didn't invent these things, of course, but that's really the point. They were so heavily invested in exploring these areas and the things they ended up saying or writing were so interesting and so skillfully infused into mythological narratives that they've survived quite prominently for millennia.

Conclusion

On a final note, there is one more thing that's important to understand about ancient Greece. Ancient Greece is technically an umbrella term that's used to lump different parts of the ancient Greek world together. Over many centuries, particularly in the period when the bulk of Greek mythology emerged and developed, the Greek world included many different city-states and polities. They are now considered to have been a common Hellenic civilization because of their shared culture and language, but the entirety of the Greek world rarely resembled a unified state. This began to change with the rise of the likes of Alexander the Great and their conquests, but the growth of Roman power would eventually put an end to unified Greek statehood in the 2nd century BC. By 146 BC, the Roman Republic absorbed the Greek city-states, ushering in a completely new era in the region.

All this is to say that Greek mythology, as described in this book, should be seen more as a collection of shared Greek traditions from the Balkans to Anatolia and beyond. The same applies especially to their religion, which is nowadays studied as one big whole made up of smaller individual parts. Since the times of Mycenae and for well over a thousand years later, various Greek centers made their own contributions and also focused on particular traditions more than others. Greeks across the region were generally familiar with the Olympian pantheon, for instance, but gods that were worshipped in one city or state wouldn't have necessarily enjoyed the same high pedestal in another.

There were also dedicated cults in different regions, which usually focused on one particular god as the main object of worship while also acknowledging the others. Ancient Greek worshipers across the region would also build temples dedicated to specific gods. In the many wars fought between various Greek states, it wasn't unheard of for belligerents to attack such sites when waging war on the other side. Despite all these variations, though, there was still a strong common thread that connected the various Greek subcultures.

As you've seen, the full diapason of Greek mythology is a rich body of myths based on a thousand years of contributions and adaptations by the Greeks themselves, which was then enriched even further by the Romans and many others. As fantastical as the stories in Greek mythology seem on the surface, perhaps the most fascinating thing about them is their timelessness and enduring relevance. From the Greek cosmogony to later stories about heroes like Hercules or Theseus, the stories are full of lessons, important questions, and themes, some more apparent than others.

Many of these themes are deeply human, and their relevance is in the fact that the subjects in the mythological narratives often ask themselves the same questions, pursue the same goals, and express the same concerns as a lot of people do even today. In that regard, the great works of ancient Greek literature are especially worth studying and unpacking. The *Iliad,* for instance, portrays the ravages of war and the destructive consequences of wrath. It comments on the nature of war and how armed conflict can sprout from the pride and ego of mortals, leading to untold suffering. These are themes that are unfortunately all too relevant today just like back then.

Then there are also the countless other themes across ancient Greek literature that are relatable on a personal level. Many of the legendary heroes often find themselves in search of meaning and purpose, asking existential questions, and fighting their own inner demons. Existential exploration has never really fallen from popularity and seems to be only gaining more traction in today's world. Exploring Greek mythology and literature in depth will reveal to you that the Greeks grappled with these issues just as much as modern humans do. It can also be refreshing and rather insightful to experience the ancient perspective on these matters.

At the end of the day, Greek mythology and its epic tales were just a stepping stone in the grand scheme of human development. Similar insights can be gained from even older writings such as the *Epic of Gilgamesh*. All of these pieces of literature and tradition offer a window into the ancient mind, and the realization of just how familiar and human that mind seems even from today's perspective can be a fascinating experience. It might also be a liberating feeling to see that people living thousands of years ago asked many of the same questions as you do now.

The truth is that some questions and components of the human condition are universal constants across time and space, consistently looming over all human affairs, no matter how different or far apart some civilizations might be. Every culture has wanted to understand where humanity comes from, why it's here, where it's going, and what's going on out there beyond the reach of human understanding and perception. The unfortunate thing is that so much of the art and philosophy that people have created while being inspired by these topics through the millennia has been lost to time.

This makes Greek mythology a priceless jewel of shared human heritage. The lengths to which the ancient Greeks went in their attempts to understand the world and the number of records preserved are all reasons why the legacy of ancient Greek culture and mythology is so enduring. A lot of that is owed to the Romans too, since they went out of their way to preserve as much as they could of the great Greek civilization that they respected so much.

For such an aggressive, expansionist imperial power, Rome showed a remarkable understanding of the value of philosophy, art, and traditions of a land that they essentially sought to conquer. Perhaps they understood over two millennia ago, just as modern anthropologists do today, that maintaining these threads of human memory was essential. The best way to fully appreciate and help maintain the enduring legacy of ancient Greece is to study it. Mythology is a key aspect of these studies, so with the detailed overview that this book has provided you, you will have quite a few paths to choose from in your pursuit of learning more about this fascinating ancient culture.

References

Cartwright, M. (2012, July 19). Hades. World History Encyclopedia; Mark Cartwright. https://www.worldhistory.org/Hades/

Cartwright, M. (2012, July 21). Jason & the Argonauts. World History Encyclopedia. https://www.worldhistory.org/article/425/jason--the-argonauts/

Cartwright, M. (2012, July 29). Greek Mythology. World History Encyclopedia. https://www.worldhistory.org/Greek_Mythology/

Cartwright, M. (2012a, July 9). Hercules. World History Encyclopedia. https://www.worldhistory.org/hercules/

Cartwright, M. (2012b, September 29). Achilles. World History Encyclopedia. https://www.worldhistory.org/achilles/

Cartwright, M. (2012c, October 21). Perseus. World History Encyclopedia. https://www.worldhistory.org/Perseus/

Cartwright, M. (2012d, December 31). Odysseus. World History Encyclopedia. https://www.worldhistory.org/odysseus/

Cartwright, M. (2016, May 2). Theseus. World History Encyclopedia. https://www.worldhistory.org/Theseus/

Cartwright, M. (2017a, March 10). Iliad. World History Encyclopedia. https://www.worldhistory.org/iliad/

Cartwright, M. (2017b, March 15). Odyssey. World History Encyclopedia. https://www.worldhistory.org/Odyssey/

Cartwright, M. (2019, September 10). The 12 Olympian Gods. World History Encyclopedia. https://www.worldhistory.org/collection/58/the-12-olympian-gods/

Cartwright, M. (2020, March 19). Orpheus. World History Encyclopedia. https://www.worldhistory.org/Orpheus/

Cartwright, M. (2013, March 7). Titan. World History Encyclopedia. https://www.worldhistory.org/Titan/

Kapach, A. (2023, February 7). Styx. Mythopedia. https://mythopedia.com/topics/styx

Kapach, A. (2023a, March 9). Chaos. Mythopedia. https://mythopedia.com/topics/chaos

Kapach, A. (2023b, March 17). Theogony. Mythopedia. https://mythopedia.com/topics/theogony

Macquire, K. (2022). The Tragic Tale of Orpheus and Eurydice. In worldhistory.org. https://www.worldhistory.org/video/2849/the-tragic-tale-of-orpheus-and-eurydice/

Macquire, K. (2022, January 27). Golden Fleece. World History Encyclopedia. https://www.worldhistory.org/Golden_Fleece/

Macquire, K., & Beck, S. (2023, April 2). The Birth of the Gods - The Ancient Greek Creation Myth. Www.worldhistory.org. https://www.worldhistory.org/video/2929/the-birth-of-the-gods---the-ancient-greek-creation/

Mark, H. W. (2022, February 21). Atreus. World History Encyclopedia. https://www.worldhistory.org/Atreus/

Miate, L. (2023, April 21). Cerberus. World History Encyclopedia. https://www.worldhistory.org/Cerberus/

Miate, L. (2023, January 16). Medea. World History Encyclopedia. https://www.worldhistory.org/medea/

Miate, L. (2023a, March 16). Gaia. World History Encyclopedia. https://www.worldhistory.org/Gaia/

Miate, L. (2023b, March 24). Uranus. World History Encyclopedia. https://www.worldhistory.org/Uranus/

Segev, M. (2018, June 1). Aristotle on Religion. Notre Dame Philosophical Reviews. https://ndpr.nd.edu/reviews/aristotle-on-religion/

Wasson, D. (2018, January 24). Oedipus the King. World History Encyclopedia. https://www.worldhistory.org/Oedipus_the_King/

Wasson, D. L. (2017, December 19). Theogony. World History Encyclopedia. https://www.worldhistory.org/Theogony/

Wasson, D. L. (2018, February 14). Medea (Play). World History Encyclopedia. https://www.worldhistory.org/Medea_(Play)/

Made in the USA
Las Vegas, NV
28 November 2024

12844014R00074